THE POWER OF
YOUR LEADERSHIP

Books by Dr. John C. Maxwell
Can Teach You How to Be a REAL Success

Relationships

25 Ways to Win with People
Becoming a Person of Influence
Encouragement Changes Everything
Ethics 101
Everyone Communicates, Few Connect
The Power of Partnership
Relationships 101
Winning with People

Equipping

The 15 Invaluable Laws of Growth
*The 17 Essential Qualities of a
Team Player*
*The 17 Indisputable Laws of
Teamwork*
*Developing the Leaders
Around You*
How Successful People Grow
Equipping 101
Intentional Living
JumpStart Your Growth
JumpStart Your Priorities
Learning from the Giants
Make Today Count
Mentoring 101
My Dream Map
Partners in Prayer
The Power of Significance
Put Your Dream to the Test
Running with the Giants
Talent Is Never Enough
Today Matters
Wisdom from Women in the Bible
Your Road Map for Success

Attitude

Attitude 101
The Difference Maker
Failing Forward
How Successful People Think
JumpStart Your Thinking
No Limits
*Sometimes You Win—Sometimes
You Learn*
*Sometimes You Win—Sometimes
You Learn for Teens*
Success 101
Thinking for a Change
The Winning Attitude

Leadership

*The 10th Anniversary Edition
of The 21 Irrefutable Laws of
Leadership*
*The 21 Indispensable Qualities of a
Leader*
*The 21 Most Powerful Minutes in a
Leader's Day*
The 360 Degree Leader
Developing the Leader Within You
JumpStart Your Leadership
Good Leaders Ask Great Questions
The 5 Levels of Leadership
Go for Gold
How Successful People Lead
Leadership 101
Leadership Gold
*Leadership Promises for
Every Day*
*What Successful People Know About
Leadership*

THE POWER
OF YOUR
LEADERSHIP

MAKING A DIFFERENCE
WITH OTHERS

JOHN C. MAXWELL

**CENTER
STREET**

NEW YORK   NASHVILLE

The author is represented by Yates & Yates, www.yates2.com.

Center Street
Hachette Book Group
1290 Avenue of the Americas, New York, NY 10104
centerstreet.com
twitter.com/centerstreet

Originally published as *Intentional Living* in hardcover and ebook in October 2015
by Center Street

First edition: October 2017

Center Street is a division of Hachette Book Group, Inc. The Center Street name
and logo are trademarks of Hachette Book Group, Inc.

The publisher is not responsible for websites (or their content)
that are not owned by the publisher.

The Hachette Speakers Bureau provides a wide range of authors for speaking
events. To find out more, go to www.HachetteSpeakersBureau.com or call
(866) 376-6591.

Library of Congress Cataloging-in-Publication Data

Names: Maxwell, John C., 1947– author.
Title: The power of your leadership : making a difference with others /
John C. Maxwell.
Other titles: Intentional living
Description: First edition. | New York : Center Street, [2017] | "Originally
published as Intentional Living in hardcover and ebook in October 2015 by
Center Street." | Includes bibliographical references.
Identifiers: LCCN 2017020195| ISBN 9781478922452 (paper over board) |
ISBN 9781546082446 (large print) | ISBN 9781478923992 (audio book download) |
ISBN 9781546082439 (spanish edition) | ISBN 9781478923985 (audio book cd) |
ISBN 9781478922469 (ebook)
Subjects: LCSH: Conduct of life. | Leadership—Religious aspects.
Classification: LCC BJ1589 .M286 2017 | DDC 158—dc23
LC record available at https://lccn.loc.gov/2017020195

ISBNs: 978-1-4789-2245-2 (hardcover), 978-1-4789-2246-9 (ebook),
978-1-5460-8244-6 (large print)

Printed in the United States of America

LSC-C

10 9 8 7 6 5 4 3 2 1

Contents

Acknowledgments

Thank you to:

Laura Morton, who sat with me for hours, asking me
questions and helping me remember my story

Stephanie Wetzel, who helped with the book's
structure and research

Charlie Wetzel, my longtime writer, who
crafted and polished the manuscript

Linda Eggers, my executive assistant, who helps me
to remain intentional every day

1

A Life That Matters

I want to start this book by asking you a simple question. Why do you want to lead others? I hope it's not for power or prestige or wealth. I hope you want to lead so that you can make a difference in the world with other people. I say that because the real power of leadership comes from what we can do with and for others. The value of leadership doesn't come from recognition. It's not about having a position. In fact, you don't need a title or designated role to work with others and lead them. Whether you're the official leader or you are just passionate about a cause, you can work with others to achieve a worthy goal.

If you want to make a difference, I hope you will find helpful guidance and inspiration in this book. The most influential leaders are powerful because of their unwavering belief in what they are trying to achieve. They have a drive to make a meaningful difference in the world; to improve the lives of countless people. They want their lives to matter, to be significant.

Is that what you want? Is there something you believe in deeply? Do you want to work with others to achieve something great? Do you want to lead a life that matters? You can. Everyone is capable of achieving great things. It doesn't matter what your age, gender, nationality, or ethnicity is. It doesn't matter how much or how little money you have. You can be a leader of change.

You don't have to be a world-class leader to connect with like-minded people to make a difference. You don't have to be a Martin Luther King Jr. or a Mother Teresa or a Nelson Mandela to be part of something significant. I hope you know that. In fact, you don't have to be a "leader" at all. Most people who make a difference don't have any kind of formal leadership position. They're just intentional—whether they are leading the team, working as part of the team, or supporting the team. One dedicated person can make a meaningful difference in the lives of others.

Anyone Can Make a Difference

I want to tell you a story that illustrates this point. In 2013 at a speaking engagement I had in Bahrain, I sat across the table from Jaap Vaandrager at lunch. He is a highly successful businessman from the Netherlands who lives and works in Bahrain. During our conversation he asked me what I was writing. I briefly shared that I was writing this book about making a difference. He responded, "My daughter Celine is making a difference in the lives of people, and she is only a teenager." He started to tell me her story, and I was blown away by it.

Growing up in the Netherlands, Celine knew how privileged she was. This became clear to her in India. Her father and grandfather had done many charity projects there, and she had gone there herself and witnessed the conditions. "I have seen how many people live in extreme poverty," said Celine. "The children in the slums and other less fortunate areas lack basic education and the only language they learn is the local language, which limits their opportunities later in life. Their greatest wish is to break out of the slums and start a life in the city with a stable job, a stable income, and a loving family."

The key, she realized, was education. "I believe that it is one of the most important things in life, and it enables people to do whatever they desire with their life," said Celine. She thought that if children could be taught English, they would have a chance at a better life as they grew up.

Celine had a plan. She would provide underprivileged children at a school with an English teacher. That would help them later in life and provide greater opportunities for them. After doing a lot of research and with the help of her friends in India, she found a school. It needed an English teacher, but didn't have enough money to pay for one. At this school and others like it, students received only the most basic supplies and a lunch, which for many is the only hot meal they get all day.

The school she found was called Mahadji Shinde Primary School. The children who attended, forty-four to a class, were some of the least fortunate children in all of India: 10 percent were orphans, 60 percent had only one parent, and 80 percent lived in sheds in the slums.

Finding an English teacher for the school was not easy, but Celine did it in a month. The teacher was a young single woman whose entire family depended on her salary, including her father who had cancer. She had been unemployed and was grateful for the job. Now all Celine had to do was figure out how to pay her.

She began raising money by holding bake sales at her school. She also sponsored swims. But the amount of money was nowhere near enough to fulfill her aims.

As Celine's sixteenth birthday approached, she knew what she wanted to do. "For my sixteenth birthday I stepped it up a notch, inviting all my friends, family's friends, and classmates to come to a birthday fund-raiser I was having, and I told them to bring a plus one."

Instead of asking for gifts, she asked for donations for a charity she was creating called No Nation Without Education.

"Within hours the whole donation box was filled and I already knew I had achieved my target," said Celine. "When I counted up the money I couldn't believe my eyes. We had... more than double the money required. Success!"

She used the money to pay the teacher's salary for a year. That meant the children would get English lessons, the teacher would have a stable job for a year, and her father's cancer would be treated. With the extra money, Celine bought dozens of basic English books for the children and stuffed animals for the primary school. When Celine went there to deliver the books and toys, the children were overjoyed and welcomed her enthusiastically. On the same trip, she helped with other projects her grandfather had sponsored.

"I had such a fantastic time in India," said Celine. "I couldn't thank everyone enough for helping me. It was a life-changing experience and one I will never forget."

But Celine's story doesn't end there. She says, "My new mission? To build a school in Mumbai, India, for my eighteenth birthday."

I wish I had read a story like Celine's when I was a teenager. Even with all of the advantages I had, no one ever pointed out that there were people doing significant things at that age. And it never occurred to me that I could make such a difference as a kid. Knowing this possibility then would have had a huge impact on me.

What's Your Story?

Everyone's life tells a story. When I meet people for the first time, as soon as the introductions are out of the way I ask them to share their stories—to tell me who they are and where they're from, where they've been and where they're going. I want to understand what matters to them. Maybe you do the same. The telling of our stories becomes an emotional connecting point for us. It bridges the gap between us.

Why is that?

Everyone loves a good story—we always have. Stories tell us who we are. They . . .

- Inspire us.
- Connect with us.
- Animate our reasoning process.
- Give us permission to act.
- Fire our emotions.
- Give us pictures of who we aspire to be.

Stories *are* us.

Every day millions of people watch movies, read novels, and search the Internet for stories that inspire them or make them laugh. Every day we listen to our friends tell us about the dramatic or funny things that happen to them. Every day people take out their smartphones to show pictures and share stories. Stories are how we relate to others, learn, and remember.

As a communicator, I spend a good portion of my days sharing stories. People don't care a lot about cold facts. They don't want to look at pie charts. They want excitement. They like drama. They care about pictures. They want to laugh. They want to see and feel what happened. Statistics don't inspire people to do great things. Stories do!

Have you ever seen the classic movie *It's a Wonderful Life*? It's the story of George Bailey, a man who dreams of traveling the world and building things, but who instead stays home in Bedford Falls, because he repeatedly chooses to do what he believes to be right for others. At one point in the movie George experiences a moment of crisis, and he comes to believe that everyone around him would be better off if he had never been born. What he's really saying is that his life doesn't matter.

The great twist in the story occurs when, with the help of an angel, George gets a chance to see what his town and others' lives would look like if he had never existed. Without him, it's a dark and negative place. George comes to recognize the positive impact he has made because, time after time, he took action to do what he knew was right and helped other people. As Clarence the angel tells him, "Each man's life touches so many other lives." George had touched many lives in small ways and made a difference.

Have you looked at your life from that angle? Have you thought about what you want your life story to be? How will your life connect with those around you? Will it make a difference?

We can't know what the future holds, but there is something you can do to make the most of your opportunities to make a difference with others. Do you know what that is?

Living each day with intentionality.

When you live each day with intentionality, there's almost no limit to what you can do. You can transform yourself, your family, your community, and your nation. When enough people do that, they can change the world. When you intentionally use your everyday life to bring about positive change in the lives of others, you begin to live a life that matters.

Get into the Story

Most people want to hear or tell a good story. But they don't realize they can and should *be* the good story. That requires you to become the leader of your own life. And it means going first, even if there isn't anyone else following you. When unintentional people see the wrongs of the world, they say, "Something should be done about that." They see or hear a story, and they react to it emotionally and intellectually. But they go no further.

Leaders who live intentionally jump in and live the story themselves. The words of physicist Albert Einstein motivate them: "The world is a dangerous place, not because of those who do evil, but because of those who look on and do nothing."

Why do so many people do nothing? I think it's because most of us look at the evils and injustice around us, and we become overwhelmed. The problems look too big for us to tackle. We say to ourselves, "What can I do? I'm just one person."

One person is a start. One person can act and make a change by helping another. One person can inspire a second person to be intentional, and another. This is where leadership begins. Helping people work together makes an impact. It can even become a movement. We should never let what we *cannot* do keep us from doing what we *can* do. A passive life does not become a meaningful life. You cannot make a difference if you stand on the sidelines.

I know that you may have a cause or a passion project you're already actively involved in. Or perhaps you possess the desire to start doing something good in your community. While my daily mission is to make a difference by adding value to leaders, yours might be raising money for the local homeless shelter or animal rescue. Maybe your dream is to help families by organizing a local food bank. Maybe you want to provide resources for special-needs children, or organize an effort to help victims of a natural disaster.

To have a life that matters, you just have to start. Start with yourself. Your *best* story begins when you put yourself back into it. Be in the picture. Stop looking— start living! And offer to help others. Not only will that change your life and positively impact others, it will grow your credibility and moral authority to inspire and lead others to make a difference.

Bringing Others into Your Story

What you move toward moves toward you. For years I have taught that when a person moves toward his or her vision, resources begin to move toward that person. Those resources may be materials, money, or people. When a person stops moving, so do the resources. As you step into your story of significance and take action, you will find this to be true.

I have taken this principle one step further by intentionally connecting with people. I don't just wait for people to move toward my vision; I invite them to join me. (I'll explain this in detail in chapter 4.) There's great power in asking others to share in your story and be part

of achieving worthy goals. Don Miller illustrates this in
A Million Miles in a Thousand Years. He writes,

> When we were in Uganda, I went with [my
> friend] Bob to break ground on a new school he
> was building. The school board was there, along
> with the local officials. The principal of the
> school had bought three trees that Bob, the gov-
> ernment official, and the principal would plant to
> commemorate the breaking of the ground. Bob
> saw me standing off, taking pictures of the event,
> and walked over and asked if I would plant his
> tree for him.
>
> "Are you sure?" I asked.
>
> "Absolutely," he said. "It would be great for
> me to come back to this place and see the tree you
> planted, to be reminded of you every time I visit."
>
> I put down my camera and helped dig the hole
> and set the tree into the ground, covering it to its
> tiny trunk. And from that moment on, the school
> was no longer Bob's school; the better story was
> no longer Bob's story. It was my story too. I'd
> entered into the story with Bob. And it's a great
> story about providing an education to children
> who would otherwise go without. After that I
> donated funds to Bob's work in Uganda, and I'm

even working to provide a scholarship to a child
I met in a prison in Kampala who Bob and his
lawyers helped free. I'm telling a better story with
Bob.[1]

When you invite others to join you, you both change
and have better stories to show for it. As poet Edwin
Markham wrote,

There is a destiny that makes us brothers
None goes his way alone.
All that we send into the lives of others
Comes back into our own.

My greatest memories have come from the times
others were in my story of significance with me. There is
no joy that can equal that of people working together for
common good. Today, my best friends are those who are
taking the significance journey with me. Those friend-
ships are heightened by meaningful experiences. Yours
will be, too.

Discoveries in Your Story of Significance

I hope you will take steps to put yourself fully into your
story and lead others to join you. From the moment you
start, it will have a positive, lasting effect on you. If

you're still not sure you're ready to take that first step, let me help by telling you what it will do for you:

It Will Change You

What is the number one catalyst for change? It's *action*. Understanding may be able to change minds, but action changes lives. If you take action, it will change your life. And that change will begin changing others.

Entrepreneur and speaker Jim Rohn said, "One of the best places to start to turn your life around is by doing whatever appears on your mental, 'I should' list." What task to help others keeps popping up on your "I should" list? I want to challenge you to develop the discipline of *doing* in that area. Every time we choose action over ease we develop an increasing level of self-worth, self-respect, and self-confidence. In the final analysis, it is often how we feel about ourselves that provides the greatest reward from any activity.

In life, it is not what we *get* that makes us valuable. It is what we *become* in the process that brings value to our lives. Action is what converts human dreams into significance. It brings personal value that we can gain from no other source.

When I was in college, I felt that I should do something positive in the poorest section of the city where I lived. Often I would hear others say that something should be done to help the people who lived there, but I didn't see anyone doing anything about it. So I decided to lead a cleanup effort in that area. For one month, volunteers did work to spruce up the neighborhood. Then we began helping the people who needed medical assistance. Soon people began to take ownership of the neighborhood, and things began to change. I vividly remember walking through that area with a great deal of pride of accomplishment. I was full of joy knowing that I had been part of a group of people who had made a difference in that community. As a result, the change inside of me was as great as the change in the neighborhood.

When you take responsibility for your story and intentionally live a life of significance, you will empower yourself, and you will grow your leadership abilities.

- *You will reaffirm your values.* Acting on what you value will clarify those values and make them a permanent priority in your life.
- *You will find your voice.* Taking action will give you confidence to speak and live out what you believe in front of others. You will begin to develop a moral authority with people.
- *You will develop your character.* Passive people allow their character to be influenced by others. Active people struggle to form and maintain their character. They grow and develop because of that struggle.

- *You will experience inner fulfillment.* Contentment is found in being where you are supposed to be. It's found when your actions are aligned with who you are.

When we live our lives intentionally for others as leaders, we begin to see the world through eyes other than our own, and that inspires us to do more than belong; we participate. We do more than care; we help. We go beyond being fair; we are kind. We go beyond dreaming; we work. Why? Because we want to make a difference.

If you want a better life, become intentional about your story and what you can achieve with and for others.

It Will Increase Your Appetite for More Significance

Celine's story shows that when you make significance a part of your story, and partner with others to achieve your goals, it only increases your appetite to do more things that matter. Celine's work to provide an English teacher and books to children in India led her to set the larger goal of building a school in India. I know that once I started adding value to others, it became an obsession in the best sense of the word. The more I did it, the more I became intentional in finding other opportunities. A butterfly cannot go back to being a caterpillar. When you start living the significance story, you get a taste for making a difference and you won't go back.

It Will Outlive You

In my book *The Leadership Handbook*, there is a chapter on legacy titled "People Will Summarize Your Life in One Sentence—Pick It Now." By getting into your story and becoming intentional about making a difference, you can choose your legacy. What an opportunity! Today you and I can decide to live a life that matters by helping others, and that will impact how we will be remembered after we're gone.

My wife, Margaret, was deeply moved by a book called *Forget-Me-Not: Timeless Sentiments for Lifelong Friends* by Janda Sims Kelley. It is a collection of prose and poetry written in the 1800s. One of the entries particularly impacted her. It said,

> *To Viola,*
> *Dare to do right, dare to be true,*
> *You have a work that*
> *no other can do.*
> *Do it so kindly,*
> *so bravely, so well,*
> *That angels will hasten*
> *the story to tell.*
> *Your friend,*
> *Annie*
> *Haskinville, New York, February 08, 1890*

Isn't that what all of us should strive to do? As Viktor Frankl said, "Everyone has his own specific vocation or mission in life. Everyone must carry out a concrete assignment that demands fulfillment. Therein he cannot be replaced, nor can his life be repeated. Thus everyone's task is as unique as his specific opportunity to implement it."

Intentional Application

What Is Motivating You?

Carefully consider the following questions and take time to write out the answers:

1. Why do you want to be a leader?
2. What are you passionate about doing to make a difference in the world?
3. Who are you willing to invite into the journey with you?

2

Why Leaders Need to Put Other People First

My start in making a difference as a leader was surely small. It happened in June 1969. In that month I graduated from college, married my high school sweetheart, Margaret, and accepted my first position as the pastor of a tiny church in rural Indiana, in a community called Hillham. The town had eleven houses, two garages, and one grocery store. Does that sound small enough?

I had high hopes and unlimited energy. I was ready to help people, so I jumped in. The first service I held in Hillham had three people in attendance. And two of them were Margaret and me!

I was not discouraged. I saw it as a challenge. I started doing what I could to help people in the community. I visited the sick, offered counseling, invited people to services, and taught messages to help people improve their lives. I did everything I knew how to do to add value to people.

Margaret and I spent three years in Hillham. Those were fantastic years. We loved the people, we learned a lot, and we worked hard. When I first accepted the position, the board offered me a part-time salary because that was all they could afford to pay, but they said I was welcome to seek additional employment at the same time if I needed to. Margaret wouldn't hear of it. "John's called to lead and grow this church, and that's what he's going to do," she told the board with all the confidence of a twenty-year-old. "I'll do the extra work." She then proceeded to juggle three jobs to help us make ends meet. She taught school, worked in a jewelry store, and cleaned houses. No doubt you can tell that I married way above myself.

Word started to spread about the good things we were doing in Hillham. People heard about our service, which had increased to 301 in attendance, and they marveled that a little country church like ours had been able to grow so dramatically. Regular attendance was so good that we had to acquire land and construct a new building to hold our growing congregation.

I was also starting to receive a positive reputation for innovation and leadership. I was getting to be known as an up-and-comer.

Moving Up

I was very pleased when I received a call from the largest church in our small denomination. They were interested in hiring me to become their new pastor. It was in Lancaster, Ohio—a big step up from tiny Hillham. We saw it as a great opportunity, so we accepted the invitation and felt we were on our way.

In Hillham I had received the inspiration to build a large church. In Lancaster I felt we would get the chance to actually do it. "We will build a great church here," I told the congregation after we arrived, and we set about doing exactly that.

Lancaster did, in fact, grow to be the church I had dreamed of. We helped a lot of people, and we made an impact on the community. It wasn't long before we were outgrowing our facilities and had to look for expansion options. We started buying up as much of the land around the church as we could. The lot closest to the church was owned by an older man named Charlie. When I first went to see him and ask about the church buying his land, he said he didn't want to sell it. "I want to die here," he told me.

I didn't pressure him. I just continued to visit him every week and build a relationship with him. After several months, one day he said, "I can tell you're helping a lot of people. Young man, I want to help you, so I am going to let you buy my land from me." So we did. And we drew up plans to build a new sanctuary and to repurpose and refurbish our existing buildings.

That same year, 1975, our church became recognized as having the fastest-growing Sunday school in the state of Ohio. That may not sound big to you, but it was huge to me. It meant my leadership had gone to another level. And people in larger pastoral circles were starting to notice, too. I was receiving recognition. It was a validation of all the hard work we were doing.

Those were heady days. My enthusiasm and emerging charisma got lots of people to join me and support my vision. And I started receiving favorable comparisons to people I admired. Because I had been born with leadership ability, I had the ability to see things before many others did, which gave me a head start in seizing opportunities and using my leadership giftedness to my advantage. I felt like I was winning all the time. And I liked it.

But there was another aspect to my personality that was threatening to limit my potential and derail me in the area of significance: my inherent competitive nature. It had been an asset when I played high school basketball, but it went to a whole new level during this season. I wanted to help people, but my motives were wrong. They were selfish. The things I was accomplishing fed my pride and my ego.

This could most easily be seen when I received the annual report of the denomination. It was a document that included the stats for every church: total attendance, percentage of attendance growth, total annual giving, number of baptisms that had been performed, number of people serving, total Sunday school attendance— everything of note that had occurred in each church during the given year. It was a snapshot of every church in the denomination.

No matter what I was doing, no matter how busy I was, no matter how important the thing I was doing might be, the moment the annual report arrived in the mail, I stopped everything. I went off with it and spent two solid days analyzing all the numbers and comparing my church's results with everyone else's.

Where do *I* rank?

How am *I* doing?

What am *I* doing well?

What do *I* need to improve?

How do *I* stand out now?

What can *I* do to stand out more?

I was obsessed with finding out where I stood in comparison with the other churches. I became completely consumed with figuring out how I could move up and keep climbing the ladder while taking our church to the next level. I didn't stop until I had every possible scenario for personal advancement figured out.

I already had an inclination to hoard good ideas, and that desire got stronger. I gave in to it. I leveraged every good idea to increase the size of my organization, and I didn't want to share my secrets with anybody else.

Why did I do all this? Because I wanted to win. I wanted to be first, and it felt like I could be first. I had the vision. I had the energy. I had the ability to attract people to myself and my cause. And I had the work ethic. When you have the potential to win, to be the best, how do you respond? Do you reach for it? I did!

However, there was a problem. You've probably already figured out what it was. It was all about me. All my goals and my desire to reach them were totally self-centered. I wasn't intentionally doing anything wrong, but my pursuit of success tainted my motives. I was in it for myself more than for others. I saw the stats as evidence of my success as a leader. I didn't care about the other churches. I didn't take into account that I was part of a larger team: the denomination. The only church I wanted to help was my own. And the only leader I wanted to win was me. I had been the high scorer for my high school basketball team, and I wanted to be the high scorer again.

While I don't think there's anything inherently wrong with achieving goals, charting progress, or tapping into natural competitiveness, I do think it's wrong to be self-centered, and that's what I was.

Shifting from Success to Significance

As I look back now, I can see that significance was beginning to be within my grasp, but instead I was reaching for success. Back then I didn't get that I couldn't have a life that mattered when it was all about me and what I accomplished. I didn't really understand that significance and the true value of leadership are about what we can do for others.

Publisher Malcolm Forbes said, "People who matter most are aware that everyone else does too." Think about this. Self-centeredness is the root of virtually every problem—both personally and globally. And whether we want to admit it or not, it's a problem all of us have.

If you're tempted to believe it's not an issue for you, then let me ask a question. When you look at a group photo that you are in, who do you look for first? You look for yourself. So do I. We all look for ourselves before we look at others. If the image of us looks good, we say, "What a great picture," no matter who else might have their eyes closed, their mouths open, or their heads turned. Our opinion is based on how good we look.

So what's the problem with being a little self-centered? From my point of view, there are many. Self-centered people don't create communities that endure. Selfishly believing that we are not our brother's keepers is not sustainable. If you want to tap into the true power of your leadership, then you need to become intentional about getting beyond yourself and putting other people first. We all do. It may not stop us completely from being selfish or from thinking of ourselves first, but it will help us to curb our self-centeredness. It will help us to shift our mind-set. It has been my observation that good leaders value people and can see the potential significance in each person.

I look back now and realize that as a young leader, I lived a very self-centered life. I had a me-first attitude that showed up in many areas of my life. My competitiveness was often unbridled, and my desire to win oftentimes overwhelmed my judgment. The thing that opened my eyes to this was a conversation with Margaret in the early years of our marriage. In those days, whenever Margaret and I disagreed, I used every skill I had to win the argument. Not just occasionally, but every time. It didn't matter if the issue was large or small, philosophical or practical, personal or organizational. Every time it was a full-court press. And I won!

Have you ever been in a situation where you lost by winning? For quite a long time, Margaret just put up with it. But then one day as I celebrated another victory, Margaret said simply, "John, you're winning the arguments, but you're losing my love."

Whoa! By winning, I was actually damaging my marriage, hurting the person I most loved. And it suddenly occurred to me that if I stayed on that same path, I had the potential to lose Margaret—the love of my life and the best gift God ever gave me.

That was a wake-up call. It opened my eyes, perhaps for the first time, to how selfish and self-centered I was. I think marriage has a way of doing that to us. If you're married, maybe you agree. At any rate, that was the beginning of change for me. I wish I could say that I instantly became unselfish and never hurt Margaret's feelings again, but that wouldn't be true. However, I can say that it began a journey of change. Whenever I felt the desire to put winning ahead of my relationship with Margaret, I was *intentional* about putting her first.

That opened the door for me, and before long I began to see my self-centeredness in other situations. So I started working on them, too. My improved attitude began to spread into these other areas of my life. As a leader, I started thinking more about others, about what they wanted and needed. You need to care about others and help them to get what they want. Do it not only because you want them to help you, but because it's the way to make a difference in the world.

I honestly didn't even notice how big a difference this was making in my life until one year when the annual report arrived in the mail. Instead of dropping everything and spending two days charting my progress, I put the report to the side and thought, *I'll look at it when I have time*. It wasn't until later that I realized the significance of that decision. I had grown. I still possessed high intensity. I was still curious about where I stood. But it no longer consumed me. Why? Because helping others and leading them had become more important. My focus had begun to shift. I was starting to become preoccupied with how to help others improve rather than with how to improve my personal position.

Tapping into Significance

What drives you when you get up in the morning? Most people settle into one of three areas: survival, success, or significance. If you're like many people, you may be struggling just to keep your head above water. You're in survival mode. Whether because of circumstances, setbacks, or poor choices, you have to put a tremendous amount of effort into just making it from day to day.

If you're working hard to make life better for yourself and your family, then I applaud you. Keep working. But once you've gotten to a place of stability, then what? What will you live for? Will you serve yourself or others? Will you put all of your energy into your own personal success, into trying to get farther ahead than others? Or will you work with others and use your leadership to help them achieve significance? Will you try to make a difference by helping others get ahead?

Much of my career as a speaker and writer has focused on helping people who have already achieved a level of success to find true meaning in their lives. For some that's a fairly smooth transition. For others it's not. Many people I interact with have gotten to a place where they've reached some of their financial goals—or surpassed them—which they thought would bring some kind of fulfillment. They went into their journeys thinking, *If I get more for me, I'll be happier.* They thought it would bring them satisfaction and fulfillment. But they've discovered that they're still not satisfied. In some cases they are actually less fulfilled than when they started their journeys. Their lives feel hollow.

Many people tie their significance to their social position, their title, their net worth or bank balance, the car they drive, their prestigious address, the man or woman on their arm, or some other status symbol. Their mentality is, *If I do enough and have enough, even if I am self-centered, it will bring fulfillment.* The problem is that self-centeredness and fulfillment cannot peacefully coexist. They're incompatible.

Sometimes people struggling with this issue are uncertain about what to do. Often, they grapple with the idea of making a career change in their forties or fifties.

When I encounter someone in this situation, I ask, "Do you really want to switch careers, or do you want to switch to a life that matters?" The problem usually isn't the job or career. When people are self-centered, they can make external changes, and they won't be any happier in their next career. No matter where they go, there they are.

Instead, they need to shift to significance by putting other people first. Their thinking needs to change from *What's in it for me?* to *What can I do for others?* Until that change occurs, happiness, fulfillment, and significance will always be out of their reach.

That doesn't mean success is bad. The reality is that people must achieve a certain amount of success before they're ready for significance. They need to have found themselves, achieved something, and made themselves valuable before they have something to give to others.

I saw this in my brother Larry. By the time he was forty years old, he had already made enough money that he would never have to work another day in his life. He once told me that his temptation was to quit working, but he knew retiring wouldn't make him happy. "So now I work for another reason," he told me. "I don't work for another home. I don't work for more money. All of the work I do now is going to allow me to give money away. I now work for a great cause—I work to help other people."

There's an important lesson here. Larry understood that he shouldn't leave his gift zone to get outside of himself. He shouldn't give up the thing he was best at, which was making money, so that he could do something else that didn't suit him, like becoming a missionary. He continued to use his talents for a better purpose. His money would work for him and become a river of influence to positively impact other people. That is true intentional living and true significance. He is living a life that matters.

Making the Shift

Like Larry, to pursue a life that mattered I had to learn to get beyond myself and think of others first. But I didn't try to get out of my strength zone. I stayed in it. I kept communicating. I kept leading. I kept rallying people to a greater purpose. I kept building. The main difference was that I was no longer doing it selfishly, self-centeredly. Maybe nobody else could tell the difference. But I could! My motives had changed.

For me, the process of changing was slow, and looked something like this:

> *I want to win.*
> *But too often I'm self-centered.*

*My bent toward competitiveness and selfish-
ness has been one of the reasons I have been successful. And my success has given me influence
and privileges. I enjoy both immensely.*

*But my success now allows me to have
options. Do I go for more success? Or do I try for
significance?*

I am at a crossroad.

*I want to use my options to add more value
to me.*

*But I also want to use my options to add value
to others.*

*What do I want my life to stand for? What do
I want it to mean?*

I will choose to help others.

The first time I chose to think of others first, it was
hard. But each time I made the right choice, it became a
little bit easier. The selfishness was still there, but over-
coming it became a little more natural. And as I became
more intentional about putting others first in my life, my
need to prove myself to others became less important.
I began to focus on putting others first—not coming in
first. I had more compelling things driving me and fulfilling me that reached far beyond me.

If you find it difficult to choose between doing what

you want for yourself and what you should do for others, don't despair. The process takes time. Think of it like an actual wrestling match. Most winning wrestlers don't end their matches instantly. They don't pin their opponents right away. They have to work at it, and eventually their opponent taps out or cries uncle. And then the match is over.

As you wrestle down your "want-tos," you don't have to give them up quickly. Just be sure that whatever you give up, you give up for the right reasons and because you've thought it through. Otherwise you will look back with regret—or worse yet, go back and try to pick them up again. It's hard to move forward with confidence if you're looking backward.

Are you ready to start putting other people first, not just occasionally, but as a lifestyle? It's not an easy shift to go from thinking of yourself first to thinking of others first. But it's an essential one for anyone who wants to transition from success to significance and live a life that matters. I started the shift in my twenties, but it took me until my thirties to really get it.

I hope you haven't waited as long as I did to serve others. But even if you have, you don't have to wait another day to change. It may take a while for you to work your way through your issues, just as I had to, but you can start the process today.

Significant leadership is always about *others*, and serving them intentionally. When you can change your thinking from *What am I going to receive?* to *What am I going to give?*—your entire life begins to turn around. And the gratification and pleasure you receive become deep and long lasting.

Intentional Application

Harness Your Success for Significance

In this chapter I discussed how my brother Larry didn't walk away from doing the things that made him successful in order to achieve significance. Instead, he shifted his focus to using his gifts and talents to benefit others.

Make a list of your top successes, your big wins based on your best skills, talents, and opportunities. You may come up with only one or two things, or your list may be quite extensive. Then think about how you could harness that success to help others. Could you use it as a springboard to help people? Could you teach others on your team how to succeed using your experience? Has it given you resources or opportunities that you could share with someone else? Should you harness your leadership by starting an organization that could make a difference? Be creative. Significance comes from using what you have to benefit others.

3

How to Begin Putting Others First

I hope by now you recognize the importance of putting other people first as a leader. But knowing what you should do doesn't always tell you *how* to accomplish it. If you want help looking beyond yourself so that you start thinking of others first, I want to give you some practical advice about how to do it. But before I do, I want to be open about what made the difference for me. It was my faith, so if that offends you, just skip ahead to my first point.

As a person of faith, I am most inspired to put others first by looking at the life of Jesus. He once asked His disciples, who were bickering over position and titles, "Who would you rather be: the one who eats the dinner or the one who serves the dinner? You'd rather eat and be served, right? But I've taken my place among you as the one who serves."[2] Jesus always valued others and always put them and their needs first.

Putting others first is at the heart of my Christian faith. Having said the Lord's Prayer more times than I can count, I have realized that the prayer is very community centered. It took me years to understand that when I said the Lord's Prayer, it wasn't about me. The focus is on *us*. Yes, if we say the Lord's Prayer, we do pray for ourselves. But we also pray for others. It's a very inclusive prayer. It is a prayer that promotes a life that matters, that leads to significance. If you've prayed the prayer, think about how it starts. It says "Our Father," and it says "give us" not "give me."

But you don't have to be a person of faith to begin putting others first. No matter what you believe, you probably sense that putting others first is the right thing to do, don't you?

Five Ways to Put Others First

If you want help taking steps away from self-centeredness and toward significance, then try doing the following:

1. Develop a Greater Appreciation for Other People

Recently I spoke at a conference for ATB Financial in Edmonton, Canada. Their top three hundred leaders had gathered for a day of leadership training, and I was their keynote speaker. They had a banner draped across the

stage that read, WHY WE LEAD—TO BRING OUT THE VERY
BEST IN OTHERS FOR OUTSTANDING RESULTS! I loved that.

During the conference, Lorne Rubis, the organization's chief people officer, instructed the attendees to ask
themselves this question: "Who brings out the best of
me?" Right alongside the others, I took his advice. For
the next thirty minutes I reflected and I wrote down the
names of people who have continually added value to
my life. Each time I added another name to this gratitude list, I would smile and remember something each
person had said or done for me that added value to my
life. My list could be endless. There isn't a week that
goes by that I don't take action on something related to
what was given to me by one of these people. One of my
greatest motivations to add value to others is to do for
others what so many have done for me.

Making such a list reminds me that I am not a self-
made man. None of us can *really* claim to have done
anything alone, can we? We need others. And we should
value them.

2. Ask to Hear Other People's Stories

In chapter 1, I talked about the importance of stories and I
encouraged you to recognize that your life can be a great
story of significance. I hope you share in that belief, and I
hope it motivates you personally. But does it motivate you
to connect with others and learn their stories?

It should, because everyone you meet has a story. We can easily lose sight of this as we go about our busy days trying to get things done. So how do we counteract this? By asking people to tell us their stories. We have to slow down and take our attention off ourselves to do that.

Do you know the stories of the people in your life? Do you know where they've come from? Are you acquainted with their struggles, their defining moments? Do you know about their hopes and dreams? Have you asked what they aspire to, and what motivates them?

It's hard to remain self-centered when your focus is on others. Hearing people's stories is a great way to get outside of yourself. Not only will their stories inspire you to help them, they will show you *ways* you can help them.

3. Put Yourself in Other People's Shoes

I read a wonderful story in the news about a couple who were in a restaurant in Iowa celebrating their anniversary. But they didn't experience the romantic evening they were hoping for. Their waiter was overwhelmed, and the service was awful. It took twenty minutes to get water, forty minutes for an appetizer, and over an hour for their entrées to arrive.

People all around them were making fun of the restaurant and how bad the service was. After taking a look around, the couple noticed their server was working twelve tables by himself. The restaurant was clearly understaffed, and he was doing the best job he could under the circumstances. Despite the slow timing, the couple realized that the waiter remained upbeat, pleasant, and apologetic throughout the meal. He was absolutely delightful.

The husband and wife, who had both been servers earlier in life, recognized that the waiter had been set up to fail, and he was trying to do his best despite that. So they left him a one-hundred-dollar tip on a sixty-six-dollar tab, along with a note that simply read, "We've been in your shoes...paying it forward."

Because this couple had done similar work to the waiter's, they had a relatively easy time putting themselves into his shoes. But you don't need to have worked a person's job to understand where he or she is coming from. You just need to make the effort to see from that person's point of view.

How often do you intentionally put yourself in other people's shoes? Do you continually try to see the world from the point of view of others? You'll be amazed by what it can do to your perspective and your attitude.

4. Place Other People's Interests at the Top of Your List of Priorities

If you get to know people, appreciate them for who they are, learn their stories, and put yourself in their shoes, then you begin to understand what their interests are. What will you do with that information? Store it away hoping to use it for leverage one day? Or put it at the forefront of your thinking every day and use it to serve them?

When we get up every day, we have one of two mind-sets. As you start your day, are you wondering what you will *reap*, or are you wondering what you will *sow*? Are you waiting for others to do something *for you*, or are you busy looking for something to do *for others*? Leaders who get outside of themselves and make a difference are looking for ways to *sow*. They put other people's interests at the top of their list of priorities every day.

5. Make Winning a Group Activity

When I started my career, I thought life was an individual hundred-yard dash. But life is really more of a relay race. While winning an individual race may feel great, crossing the finish line with your team is better. Not only is it more fun, but it's also more significant.

John Wooden, who mentored me for many years, said, "Selfishness is the greatest challenge for a coach. Most players are more concerned with making themselves better than the team." The result? Seldom do the best players make the best team. Wooden described an unselfish player as one who "showed an eagerness to lose himself to the group for the goal of the team." Not only does that describe a good team member and a good leader, but it also describes an intentional person who lives a life that matters by making a difference.

Change Yourself before Expecting Change in Others

Before we leave the subject of getting outside of yourself and putting others first, I feel that I should caution you about a potential pitfall you may face as you make this shift—the desire to change other people.

When I first started out in my career, I thought that helping people meant trying to change them. So I made that my goal. I wanted to teach messages that would take people to a higher place in their lives. I gave lots of advice. I was young and idealistic. I didn't yet understand that people don't change because you want them to. They change because they want to, and it happens only when they're ready to.

What I missed was that the first person we need to change is *ourselves*. Self-leadership always comes first. It is the prerequisite for leading others. If we want to change the world, then we must change. People can't be agents of change unless they've gone through positive change themselves. I learned that I had to travel within before I traveled without. In other words, I had to make some changes in myself before I could expect to effect change in others. I could not give what I did not have.

If I wanted to see others transformed, I had to be transformed. I had to do the hard work myself.

This ultimately contributed to my shift from teacher to leader. I realized that if I changed, then put others' needs above my own and cared more about their wants than my own, I could make an impact. I could speak as a friend, as one who had been in the trenches, who had been where they are.

It is also one of the reasons that when I speak today I use so many personal illustrations. I know it's the most effective way to connect with people. All of my conviction and confidence comes from talking about things that happened to me. When I speak about my experiences, people relate mine to how their own experiences have affected them.

The power of personal transformation to help others can be seen in Global Teen Challenge, an organization that helps kids get off drugs. I serve on an advisory board to them, and when I hear the stories of transformation, it amazes and inspires me. Their organization's success rate is nearly 70 percent, while that of others trying to do the same things is closer to 18 percent.

Curious about the staggering difference, I asked the president of Global Teen Challenge about it at one of our meetings. He responded, "Almost all the people that do the teaching for Global Teen Challenge are former drug addicts. We don't bring in people who have studied the drug issue. We don't bring in educators to talk to people. There's tremendous change that happens in someone's life when the person who's trying to help them out of the ditch had to get out of the ditch him- or herself."

There is an amazing amount of motivation, hope, and credibility when someone has been there, done that, and gone on to become successful. If the person telling you to get off drugs hasn't been through the experience, there's no common ground—or credibility. If they have done drugs, yet kicked the habit, they stand on higher ground saying, "Come up to where I am standing." We lead better when it's from experience.

But the key change is not just in our experiences or our decisions. What really needs to change are our hearts. What must transform are our attitudes. What must be purified are our motives. We can't allow our lives to be all about us. That's not the way to do something that makes a difference. It's not the way to lead others. If we want to choose significance, to be effective leaders, we must put other people first.

Making It a Priority to Put Others First

After I served in my second leadership role in Lancaster, I spent almost two years working in Indiana, which I'll talk about in chapter 6, and then I became the senior pastor at Skyline, a church in the San Diego area. I spent fourteen years there, and I loved it. We made a

positive impact on our community. We donated significant amounts of money to the county for projects every
year. And we led many people to lives of significance. In
addition, people came from all over to visit the church,
attend services, and worship among the thousands of
congregants. Wherever I traveled, people would say,
"This is one of the most influential pastors in the country." In the eyes of many, I had reached the pinnacle of
success as a pastor.

While I was appreciative of the opportunities I'd
been given throughout the years, and was grateful to be
included in the company of leaders I viewed as better,
faster, and smarter than I was, I had a sense that I could
make an even greater impact. I felt I could be more significant by serving and adding value to people outside
the church than I could if I remained in the pastorate.

I recognized I could no longer hold on to all I had if
I wanted to move on, serve more people, and do bigger
things. I knew it would be impossible to keep leading
Skyline and help even more people outside the church at
the same time. I couldn't do both with excellence.

This wouldn't be an easy decision. All my life I had
been able to point to something tangible as a symbol of
my success. I worried that if I left the church, I would no
longer have that, and the loss of this aspect of my personal identity gave me great hesitancy about resigning.
However, I knew that I wanted to go toward my higher

calling, where I knew I could serve others and make a difference. So I tendered my resignation at Skyline, and I started to focus my attention on putting others first by training leaders across the country.

I had been leading leadership conferences for fourteen years by that time, and I noticed that more and more businesspeople had begun showing up to learn from me, even though the conferences were designed primarily for church leaders. So I knew I would continue teaching leadership, but I started to make it more inclusive.

At this time I also put more focus on writing books. I wanted to make a difference in the lives of people I would never get to meet or who would not attend my conferences. I began partnering with Charlie Wetzel as my writer. Since then, he and I have written nearly ninety books together.

The second area where I put more energy was in helping other church leaders raise money for building projects. One of the things I had done not only at Skyline but also in Lancaster and Hillham was raise money to construct new buildings and relocate our growing congregations. I remember thinking to myself, *If I can raise millions of dollars for my church, what would happen if I started a company that could help churches and pastors all over America to do that?* I started another company and hired some good leaders I knew to become consultants to churches. Those consultants served many pastors and their churches. Together, we helped churches to raise $3 billion.

But perhaps the most significant change I made came when my brother Larry and I founded the nonprofit organization EQUIP. The seed for the idea was planted in 1985, when I was thirty-eight years old. I was coming home from a trip to Peru, where I had spent a week speaking to a group of American translators. They were a group of very smart and talented people, but they were consumed with their work. They were in leadership positions, and I spoke to them about improving their leadership skills, but they weren't especially responsive to my message, and, frankly, I was frustrated by their lack of interest in the help I was trying to offer them. They couldn't see beyond their pressing responsibilities to learn something new that would help them improve their leadership skills.

On the flight home, I turned to Margaret and said, "I don't want to speak in other countries anymore. In America I can use all of my tools to impart what I've learned. I can fall back on my sense of humor to teach my leadership principles and get a response from nearly any audience. Whenever I speak internationally, the response is slow at best because there are cultural differences. It's hard work. I don't need to work that hard! I think I'll stay home."

Margaret responded by asking, "Is there a need to raise up solid leaders around the world?"

"Of course," I replied.

"Do you believe that you can help them become better leaders?"

"Yes," I answered, "but it's a slow, laborious process and it's not what I like to do."

"John, God didn't give you your gifts for you to please yourself. He gave them to you to help others."

Wow! Those words hit me in the gut. The moment she said it, I knew she was right. I needed to put other people's needs ahead of my own.

I dropped the subject in our conversation, but I could not get rid of it in my mind. For the next several days I mentally and spiritually wrestled with the selfishness of my heart. I knew what I *should* do, and boy, was it at odds with what I *wanted* to do.

This wasn't going to be a situation where I could make a list of pros and cons and act on whichever column had more items listed. I knew the importance of the individual pros would have greater weight than the sheer number of cons. No matter how much I wanted to stay in my comfort zone, stay away from unfamiliar food, rely on my American humor, and stick with the relative ease of traveling within my own country, I had to face a decision.

When I did sit down with a legal pad in my favorite thinking chair, I listed more than a dozen reasons why I didn't want to teach internationally on my con side of the list. On the pro side, there were only two:

1. It was the right thing to do.
2. I couldn't ignore my true calling.

In the end, I knew that if I didn't follow through, the loser would be me. Why? Because I wouldn't be doing the one thing I had committed myself to—adding value to the lives of others. I had never put conditions on where people had to live when I made that commitment. If I wanted to reach my significance potential, I needed to be willing to put others first.

From that time, I began to accept more invitations to teach leadership outside the United States. But my commitment to serving others outside the United States didn't go to the next level until Larry and I founded EQUIP, a nonprofit dedicated to training leadership internationally.

Now, two decades later, I can look back and say that it's been an amazing journey. We have trained five million leaders from every country in the world. And today we're making efforts to put others first by teaching values, which we hope will transform nations.

Remember, Everyone Starts Small

One of my worries about telling you my story is that it might sound bigger and better than it really is. Don't forget that I started out in Hillham, and I spent twenty-six years working to add value to people before Larry and I started EQUIP. Is it true that EQUIP has trained more than five million people? Yes. Do Larry and I deserve the credit for that? No. It is the result of hundreds of volunteers and thousands of donors. We owe a lot to the original board of directors who bankrolled the entire organization, and to subsequent board members who supported the vision mentally, emotionally, spiritually, and financially. Because they put others first and provided leadership to make a difference, we have been able to serve many people.

You don't have to have an organization to put others first. And you don't have to want to do big things. Doing something for one person is big. The point is to get started and serve others. You can do that, and you can start today.

Intentional Application

Look for Clues in People's Stories

Do you know the stories of the people in your life? Not just the stories of close family members, but also of your employees, co-workers, clients, neighbors, and friends? If not, make it your goal to ask at least one person to tell you his or her story this week and every week until you've heard them all. Listen not only to learn their histories, but also to discover their hopes, dreams, and aspirations. Make notes if needed to help you remember. And try to identify specific ways you would be able to make their interests one of your priorities. It's difficult to put others first when you don't know them or what they care about.

4

Connecting with Like-Minded People

It is a fact that no person can achieve great things alone. It's never been done, nor will it ever be. People try to achieve significance by themselves mainly because of the size of their ego, their level of insecurity, their temperament, or simple naïveté. But it can't be done. That was a painful lesson I only needed to be taught once as a young leader. You may be able to achieve some degree of success by yourself, though even that is difficult. But it is impossible to live a life that matters and find significance without other people.

Attracting People to a Cause

I have always been keenly aware that I have the kind of personality that attracts people to me and to whatever I'm excited about. The authors of the assessment tool

StrengthsFinder call this "woo." While I was at Lancaster, I used this ability heavily. In fact, as soon as I realized that I needed to make a difference *with* people to achieve significance—instead of trying to make a difference *for* people—I started recruiting everybody I could to partner with me. I immediately began asking others to join my team. I became an Uncle Sam of significance. Everywhere I went, I pointed to everyone I saw and said, "I Want You."

In those days, I had dreams of being a positive influencer in our small town of Lancaster, Ohio. I wanted to build a large auditorium to house our growing congregation. I needed to start social programs to help people in need. I had a great desire to host leadership conferences to help others lead more successfully. My dreams were bigger than me, but they certainly weren't out of reach. True significance will always be bigger than the person with the dream. That's why it requires a team of people working together to achieve it.

I began to share my dream with anyone and everyone to see what it did to them. Whenever I spoke, I talked about my dream. If someone stopped me on the street or at the mall, he heard about my dream. If somebody passed me in a hallway, she heard my dream. I was looking for people with a heart to make a difference and who could make things happen. I was developing a leadership track, believing that people who could produce results could always get the job done. That didn't mean I only recruited leaders, but I felt certain if people could make good things happen for themselves, they could make positive things happen for others. I believed that if you have the heart to make a difference, there is always an answer, but if you have a heart of indifference, there is never an answer.

As I spread the word about what I wanted to do and how I wanted to include others, many people joined me. I was passionate, and passion is contagious. And that's a good thing because it takes a lot more energy to do something for other people than for ourselves. The good news is that I was moving from *me* to *we* during this time. But I still had a lot to learn.

Many people eagerly climbed aboard the Maxwell train. I thought that was success. It took me a couple of years to figure out that the people who were joining me in the early days just wanted to come along for the ride. They liked my enthusiasm and energy, and they wanted to be close to me, but they didn't necessarily share the same passion I had for significance, for making a difference with others. They just wanted to hang out. They didn't have the same goal or purpose I did. We were on the same train but wanted to go in different directions.

At first I thought the problem was that they were on the *wrong* train. Instead of asking, "What can we do for others?" they were asking, "What can you do for me?" But then it dawned on me—they weren't on the wrong train. I had simply recruited the wrong people. I should have checked their tickets. I should have shared the purpose of the journey I was taking before I said, "All aboard!"

This required another shift in my thinking and a change in the way I led people. I had to stop the proverbial train and allow everyone who wasn't holding the right ticket to get off. Then I had to proactively go out and attract the *right* people and begin the journey again.

You may find this to be true of your own goal. There may be people who are drawn to you by your passion for something instead of having their own passion for the mutual goal. So how can you recognize the right people?

For me, they were people who were already working toward the goal. They were the people already actively making a difference in the lives of others, not just wanting to hang out with those who were making a difference. There is a big difference between the two. When you surround yourself with people who share your vision and purpose, people who crave and are willing to work toward your common goal, there is always a way to achieve your purpose, no matter the obstacles.

How was I going to connect with these people? I realized I needed to have a clearer picture of what I was trying to accomplish. I needed to get clarity for myself and for my cause. Once I got that, I could declare it to others and see how they would respond.

Articulating a Dream

So I took the next six months to carefully construct a statement describing what I was seeking. It became my own version of "I Have a Dream," inspired by the speech of the great Martin Luther King Jr. Certainly my version was not as good as his—how could it be? But it was the best I could make it. It took me *at least* fifty drafts before I finally got it to be a version I could live with. It was my first attempt at writing a vision statement that I thought would attract the right kind of people into my world, people who shared my passion to make a difference for others, and it stuck for a very long time.

Here's what I wrote:

I Have a Dream

History tells us that in every age there comes a time when leaders must come forth to meet the needs of the hour. Therefore, there is no potential leader who does not have an opportunity to better mankind. Those around him also have the same privilege. Fortunately, I believe that God has surrounded me with those who will accept the challenge of this hour.

My dream allows me to . . .

1. Give up at any moment all that I am in order to receive all that I can become.

2. Sense the invisible so I can do the impossible.

3. Trust God's resources since the dream is bigger than all my abilities and acquaintances.

4. Continue when discouraged, for where there is no faith in the future, there is no power in the present.

5. Attract winners because big dreams draw big people.

6. See myself and my people in the future. Our dream is the promise of what we shall one day be.

Yes, I have a dream. It is greater than any of my gifts. It is as large as the world but it begins with one. Won't you join me?

I took what I wrote to a print shop and had it printed on laminated five-by-seven-inch cards so that I could hand them out. I gave hundreds of cards to people.

Anytime I sensed that someone might be seeking significance, I gave him or her a card.

When I gave it to people, there was no pressure, no strings attached, and no cultish sales pitch. All I did was hand them a card and say, "Read this. If you want to join me, let me know." If they asked questions, I took no more than a couple of minutes to share my dream of significance with them. Every time someone reached out their hand, without realizing it they were accepting a little piece of me into their lives. Hundreds and eventually thousands of people joined me.

It turned out that my "I Have a Dream" card was an important piece of my significance journey because it told people who I was, what I did, and what I wanted to accomplish. It was a tangible way to express what I felt, to put my ideas out there and quickly identify like-minded people who would want to join me.

Remember, after I figured out that I needed to consider who I was recruiting, I didn't give the card to just anyone. I only handed it to those I felt shared my mindset. I used it selectively, and when I did, it was an easy way to say, "The ball is in your court." Happily, the majority of those I chose to give the card to took that ball, looked me straight in the eyes, and said, "Count me in!" Now, that's what I call getting in the game.

I intuitively knew that the way I wrote my dream card would appeal to the right people, because the wording was deliberate and meant to be an intentional elimina-tor. Why? Because my "I Have a Dream" was really a challenge. You see, great vision is a separator: People who migrated toward the vision wanted significance. Those who backed away from it wanted something else, which was fine. I didn't want to partner with people who didn't share my vision.

I continued to print these cards and hand them out for two years. And I knew something special was hap-pening when reactions started to change from "Sure, I'll take this card," to "Do you mind if I keep this?" I never once asked anyone to join me. I just gave out the cards and said, "Think about it. Get back to me." I left the decision in their hands. And I was attracting the exact people I'd been looking for.

If you want to make a difference with people, you just need to find like-minded people who share common goals for doing something significant. You just need to want to make a difference together and then do it!

Factors That Connect People of Significance

My wish for you is that you connect with people who will go with you on your significance journey. I want you to work with like-minded people, those who share your passion to make a difference in the world. And I believe you can.

To help you with that, allow me to show you nine factors that attract people of significance to one another. These observations are based on my version of "I Have a Dream." To explain how this works, I'll break what I wrote for my card into sections and explain each of them in turn. They will help you as you seek like-minded people in search of significance.

1. The Opportunity Factor

History tells us that in every age there comes a time when leaders must come forth to meet the needs of the hour. Therefore, there is no potential leader who does not have an opportunity to better mankind. Those around him also have the same privilege.

Significant acts almost always occur in response to opportunities. What opportunities do you see? Do you see a way to connect others to your mission? Or is someone inviting you to join him or her in doing something significant? If you see it, seize it. What you say yes to shapes your life. Sometimes the smallest step in the right direction ends up being the biggest step in your life. Tiptoe if you must, but take that first important step.

Question: What opportunity do you see right now to make a difference?

2. The Belief Factor

Fortunately, I believe that God has surrounded me with those who will accept the challenge of this hour.

If you don't believe in God, I don't have any desire to push my personal beliefs or faith on you. I place no judgment on anyone. I know without a doubt that every day since I started asking God to bring me people who desired significance, He has been sending them into my life so that we could make a difference together. And God continues to send them.

But you don't have to believe in God to believe that like-minded people will come into your life when you have it in your heart to do something meaningful. Do you believe that? Do you believe others want to connect with you to make a difference? When someone who wants to make a difference comes across your path, do you recognize him or her? Do you believe enough in that person to connect with him or her and to start thinking about what you might do together to make a difference? Belief is essential for creating significant change. Without belief, you will have a very difficult time leading the way to make meaningful change happen.

Question: Do you believe people are coming to you to help you make a difference?

3. The Possibility Factor

My dream allows me to give up at any moment all that I am in order to receive all that I can become.

The pathway of possibility is filled with trade-offs. Why? Because there is no significance without sacrifice. But the good news is that as you trade one thing for another, you will be moving toward a better and more fulfilling way of life. This isn't true just of leadership, but of life. Consider the sacrifices that come with all the benefits of starting a family or making radical changes to your everyday life.

Each of us is faced with moments in life where we are forced to stop, reflect, and consider our options. Nearly every choice is a trade-off, and we start making them early in life. Will we watch television shows or play outside? Will we play in high school or work to get good grades? Will we take a job when we finish high school to make some money right away, or will we go to college? When we graduate, will we take the job that pays more money or will we choose the one that will give us better experience?

As a leader, you will be constantly faced with decisions, and many will not be easy. Choosing one path usually means sacrificing something else. And know this: the more successful you are, the greater and more challenging the trade-offs will be that you have to make. If you want to lead in a way that matters, you will have to make trade-offs. And they become harder as we become more successful. But know this: trade-offs never leave you the same. And if you trade up for significance over serving yourself, those changes will always be for the better.

Question: What are you willing to give up to make a difference?

4. The Faith Factor

My dream allows me to sense the invisible so I can do the impossible. Trust God's resources . . .

Again, I frame this in the context of my faith, but the issue here is really about fear. Almost everything you and I want is on the other side of fear. How do we handle that? How do we get beyond our fears?

For me it's a faith issue. I try to leave everything in God's hands, and I usually see God's hand in everything. I don't believe God gives me a dream to frustrate me. He gives me a dream to be fulfilled.

Do you want to know something amazing? Fear is the

most prevalent reason why most people stop. Faith is what makes people start. Fear is the key that locks the door to the resources. Faith is the key that opens that door.

If you are motivated by a dream of significance that is right for you, it should increase your faith. You should believe your dream *can* be accomplished, and that you are leading others in the right direction. Faith should help you see the invisible and do the impossible. It should help release the resources you need. Even if you have a different kind of dream from mine, I believe you can trust God's resources.

The faith factor encourages me to start walking and to believe the resources will come to me as I walk. I know they will not come if I sit still. If I stop, the resources stop. Resources come to us when we are on our missions, when we are fulfilling our callings.

The lesson I teach most often on faith is this: feed your faith and starve your fear. To do that you must give your faith more energy than your fear. You can't reduce fear by thinking about it. You reduce it by taking action away from it. How? By moving toward faith.

Faith does not make things easy, but it makes things possible because it puts everything, including fear, into the right perspective. So if you want to become a stronger leader—to learn, to grow, to achieve your dreams of significance, and to make a difference—have faith.

Question: Is my faith greater than my fear?

5. The Challenge Factor

... the dream is bigger than all my abilities and acquaintances.

Sometimes I think there are no great men or women. There are just great challenges that ordinary people like you and me are willing to tackle. Why do I say that? Because nothing separates passionate people from passive people like a call to step up. Whenever I invite others to join me in doing something big by casting a vision of significance, I realize that some people will respond positively to it and others will run from it.

Today I feel more challenged to make a difference than at any other time in my life. It is my passion to raise up people as intentional leaders so that they will rise up and become transformational leaders. As I have studied movements of transformation, I have endeavored to define what a transformational leader looks like. I believe transformational leaders influence people to think, speak, and act in such a way that it makes a positive difference in their lives and in the lives of others. It's my dream—and my challenge—to develop transformational leaders. It's much easier to define one than it is to develop one. However, I have accepted the challenge.

My hope is that this book will help you to move in this direction—to become intentional in making a difference, and to help take others there as well. If you and I do that and help others to do the same, we can help transform individuals and communities.

Question: Are you challenged to stretch to significance?

6. The Attitude Factor

My dream allows me to continue when discouraged, for where there is no faith in the future, there is no power in the present.

I've always been impressed by the leadership of Martin Luther King Jr. He was able to inspire so many people to perform significant acts during his relatively short lifetime. It led to a movement that created positive change for America. King once said, "The biggest job in getting any movement off the ground is to keep together the people who form it." I believe a big part of his success in doing that came from his attitude. He never seemed to lose hope. He kept believing in the change he was working toward, up to the very end of his life.

When I lived in Atlanta, I had the privilege of meeting numerous people who both marched with Dr. King and were jailed with him. They overcame a lot to make a difference for those who came behind them. And while

King was alive, he kept them together. He helped people to keep their attitudes like his.

I've often wondered why so many good people stop doing good things in their lives. I've concluded that people lose energy not because the work they do is hard, but because they forget why they started doing it in the first place. They lose their *why* and as a result, they lose their way. When their attitudes slip, so do their efforts.

I believe most people who try to make a difference start out with the right motives and attitudes. As a result, the people they help gain a tremendous amount from them. But what often starts to occur is a shift in thinking, from *I want to help people* to *I want people to help me*. This is especially destructive when this shift occurs in the leaders. The moment that transition in attitude takes place, the leaders' motives change. Instead of enlisting people to whom they can add value and who will join them in adding value to others, the leaders want to attract people who can add value to *themselves*.

When people are motivated by personal advantage, they've lost their way. As a result, they get off track and they can no longer make a difference. When you stop loving people, you stop serving them well. If you're wondering, *Why aren't others serving me?* it becomes a source of discontent. And if you're a leader, you forfeit your leadership effectiveness.

Attitude so often is the difference maker. I had a

friend who once said to me, "When life is sweet, say thank you and celebrate. When life is bitter, say thank you and grow." That's a great attitude. And it's the kind of attitude required to make a difference and connect with other difference makers.

And let me say one more thing about attitude. It's easy to have a good attitude when life is good. The time a positive attitude really counts is when things are going badly. We don't always choose what happens to us, but we can always determine how we respond. When we choose the right attitude even when things are going wrong, that is highly attractive and appealing to the people who partner with us.

Question: Is your attitude an asset or liability?

7. The Winning Factor

My dream allows me to attract winners because big dreams draw big people.

When I wrote the above sentence for my "I Have a Dream" card, I can remember how I felt. The dream that I possessed thrilled me, but it had not yet attracted many people who could help me achieve it. I wanted to connect with people motivated by significance who could make things happen. But I also wondered how such people might react to my invitation.

Would they understand my dream?

Would my dream widen the gap between them and me?

Would they criticize it?

When I looked at the people I knew, I was tempted to keep my dream to myself. Sharing a dream that has deep personal meaning is a risk. It can invite ridicule or rejection. But I also knew that if I wanted to achieve the goal of making a difference, I had to connect with good people so that we could work together. So I gathered my courage, took a leap of faith, and made the decision to tell others.

The responses I received were varied and interesting. Most people fell into one of three categories: survival, success, and significance. People interested only in survival hid. They wanted no part of my vision. Some people who were seeking success bought in. But the ones who most readily connected were those who wanted significance. Big dreams draw people with potential who want to jump in the deep end, way over their heads, and learn to swim.

Another discovery I made while sharing my dream was surprisingly delightful. Dreams often come one size too big so that we can grow into them. It's like when I was a child and my parents always bought my shoes half a size too big. They would say, "John, you're growing. You're becoming a young man. You will grow into these in no time."

That's what I now say to people when they first put on their significance shoes. They may feel a little too big for you at the moment, but don't worry. As you start taking steps, you will grow into them and become the significant person you were created to be.

Are you taking the risk of sharing your dream with others? And are talented, successful, motivated people connecting with you so that you can try to achieve those dreams together? You need those winning kinds of people to make a difference. And you need to *be* one of those winners yourself!

When it comes to significance, I still feel like I'm wearing shoes that are too big and I need to grow into them. I'm still in over my head and trying to swim. And that's good. I'm getting older in years, but younger in my dreams. That's what makes me love this journey I'm on.

Question: Are you connecting with winners to achieve significance?

8. The Promise Factor

My dream allows me to see myself and my people in the future. Our dream is the promise of what we shall one day be.

When I wrote this phrase, I truly believed a worthy dream contained a promise of its fulfillment. But that was a naive mistake. I had made the same mistake most people make about dreams. I thought, *If you believe it, you can achieve it.* But that's not always true. A dream requires a partner: commitment.

Dreams are free. However, the journey to fulfill them isn't. You have to work for your dream. Your dream doesn't work for you. You have to work with the dream and for the dream. The dream is a *promise* of what you can be, but *commitment* is the reality of what you will become. What starts as a promise ends as a commitment.

Question: Have you committed to a path with great promise for you and others?

9. The Invitation Factor

Yes, I have a dream. It is greater than any of my gifts. It's as large as the world but it begins with one. Won't you join me?

We all have a certain amount of luck in our lives, but the best luck is what I like to call "who luck." Why? Because *who* you connect with matters the most. The "who luck" in your life can be either good or bad, depending on who joins you. I'm sure you know that instinctively. Haven't you met people who worked with you who made it easier for both of you to make a difference? And haven't you also connected with people you later wished you'd never met—because they hindered your ability to make a difference? I have.

All my life I've looked for ways to connect with others, as a church leader, a business leader, and a communicator. But you don't have to be a leader to invite people to something of significance. You just need to be committed to your cause and open to working with others to achieve it. If you think leadership is getting people to follow you, you may be a good leader. But if you think leadership is getting people to follow a great cause, you have the potential to be a great leader. If your *why* is big enough to excite you, then, as you share it, it will excite others—especially those who share your passion and dream. The size of your *why* will determine the size of your response.

Question: Are you ready to start inviting others to join you in living a life that matters?

Right now are you only dreaming about making a difference, or are you actually doing things to connect with people who can join you on the significance journey? Movements don't begin with the masses—they always start with one, and then they attract others to themselves and their causes. That was the case in the antiapartheid movement in South Africa. In 1941 this is what South African anti-apartheid activist Walter Sisulu wrote about Nelson Mandela: "We wanted to be a mass movement and then one day a mass leader walked into the office."

Intentional Application

What Is Your Dream?

Most people who would like to do something significant have ideas and intentions, but they rarely have specific, vivid pictures of their dreams written out. That lack of clarity makes it more difficult for them to achieve their dreams—and to connect with other like-minded people who would be interested in partnering with them to accomplish those dreams.

Take some time to write out your dream. It can contain your principles, as mine did. It can contain specifics, as Martin Luther King Jr.'s did. It can be a poem, a story, a list. Make it your own, but be sure to *write it down*. You may be able to write it in a sitting. Or it may take you months, as it did me. That's not important. The process of writing it forces you to clarify your thinking and know what you want.

Once it's done, you can decide who to share it with. I know it may seem risky and it may make you feel vulnerable, but you need to start telling others about your dream for making a difference. Begin sharing it with people who will encourage you, whether or not they are likely to join you. Then widen your circle. Begin telling people whom you believe to be like-minded, and see where it leads.

5

Adding Value from Your Sweet Spot

It was the worst day of my young life as a pastor. Benny Harris, a board member and leader of the Hillham congregation, called me in Lancaster to share with me that my former church in Hillham was not doing well. Six months after I had left, the attendance had fallen from three hundred to less than a hundred. Benny's voice was broken as he asked, "What's gone wrong?"

I had no answers for him. And I felt empty for not knowing how to respond.

I went outside and walked around trying to clear my head. I felt terrible. I kept asking myself the same question: *What went wrong?*

When I made the transition from the small church in Hillham to the larger church in Lancaster, I felt very satisfied and proud of my accomplishments at that first church. My reputation in the small Hillham church was like that of Superman, leaping tall buildings and growing the congregation from the ground up—from three to over three hundred.

I had worked so hard to grow the congregation. I had cared for those people as well as I could. A beautiful new church building had been built on a knoll, and it was filling up week after week before I left. Why was it slowly emptying after my departure? My sense of prideful self-satisfaction came crashing down quickly.

What happened? I wondered.
How could it all fall apart so fast?
Why did it fall apart?
Who was to blame?

In my early twenties, I was long on energy but short on practical experience. It took me six months of thinking through all the possibilities of what went wrong, until it hit me like a ton of bricks. I finally figured out the problem. And when I did, I became even more discouraged by the realization.

The problem was me!

Have you ever racked your brain to solve a problem only to discover that you were the cause? There is nothing worse than that. But that was where I found myself.

What happened was actually a common rookie leadership mistake. I had done all the work myself in that little church. Well, not just me. Margaret and I did the work. She handled the youth, missions, special projects, and hospitality. I led the church, preached, visited people, recruited new people, developed programs, and handled problems.

As the congregation grew, I felt like a local rock star. My Volkswagen Beetle ran nonstop on those dusty dirt roads doing "God's business" for the community. People were enthralled by my boundless energy, wondering, "How does he get it all done?" As my reputation got bigger, unfortunately, so did my head. When pastors asked me how I was developing that little country church, I would proudly say, "I work hard." Then I would go into great detail about the importance of working longer hours, putting in sweat equity, and paying the price if they wanted to build a great church.

I didn't have a clue. I'm embarrassed by that now.

Never once did I invest in people. I had loved the people, but I had never added value to them. After I left Hillham, many people were really no better off than they had been before I arrived there.

I hadn't trained anyone to take over in my absence. While I was busy building my career, I didn't include other people along the way. Everyone around me was happy to let me do it all. More than that, they *loved* me for it. And I gladly accepted the applause because

I thought that was what a good leader was supposed to do—work harder than everyone else and accept the accolades.

Boy, was I wrong. I had built everything around *myself*, so when I left, it all fell apart. It was a fast fall, too. I didn't realize what I had done until after I got the news from Benny. It was a result of my inexperience and naïveté.

After licking my ego wounds for a few weeks, I had to figure out how to begin to fix what was broken in me. I didn't want to continue making the same mistakes as I went forward. Anything of real significance is lasting. It doesn't fall apart quickly once it no longer has your attention. That's especially true if you're a leader. The true measure of success is succession—what happens after you're gone.

I started to think about what I needed to do. The first step in my recovery was clear. I had to admit to myself that I was not indispensable. And I had to stop doing things that made me *feel* indispensable. I needed to shift my focus. Instead of making a difference *for* people, I would work to make a difference *with* people. Instead of doing things to emphasize my value, I would focus on making others more valuable.

The pathway seemed clear to me. I would start by equipping people so that no matter what happened to me, they could carry on and make a difference. I would ask others to join me in doing the work and in leading, and I would add value to them. That would not only show them that I cared for them, but also help to develop them as individuals, improve their quality of life, and give them new skills that would benefit them, the organization, and others.

Although the shift from making a difference *for* people to making a difference *with* people may sound like a subtle switch in behavior, it was actually a radical shift in my approach. When I arrogantly thought I was the entire picture, I could never see the bigger picture. But once I realized that my focus needed to be on others and on adding value to them, I was able to multiply my impact, fine-tune my purpose, and work within my best gifts.

Becoming Intentional in Adding Value

If you want to be significant and lead in a way that matters, you must add value to others. I know I'm repeating myself, but I have to say it again: significance and selfishness don't go together. You cannot be a selfish, self-centered person and be a good leader. You have to take the focus off yourself and put it on making the lives of others better.

What you must do to be significant is consistent for everyone. You must add value. *How* you do that is as unique as you are. It begins with figuring out your purpose. And it continues with your unique gifts and talents, opportunities and resources. My two greatest gifts are communication and leadership. Where those two intersect is where I add the most value. It's my sweet spot. Why do I communicate? To add value to people. Why do I lead? To add value to people. That's how I make a difference.

When someone comes to me and says he wants to become a leader, one of the first questions I ask is, why? Why do you want to become a leader? Is it because you want a corner office? Is it for a premium parking place or a top salary? Is it for the perks and recognition? All of these are wrong motives. People who want to become leaders for any reason other than adding value are way off base.

For most people who don't add value to others, their actions aren't motivated by hate or even self-centeredness—they're usually caused by *indifference*. However, no one can be indifferent and live a life of significance. We have to *want* to make life better for others to make a difference.

Many people approach this too casually. They are prompted by circumstances. They see a person in trouble and stop to help. Or a friend calls needing assistance and they respond. That's good. But there is another, higher level of adding value that significant people embrace. It's intentional. It's proactive. It's a lifestyle.

Leaders who have a meaningful impact on others make it their everyday goal to add value to people using their best gifts, skills, and resources. It's part of their *purpose*. They are always actively looking for ways to make the lives of other people better. That's both a responsibility of leadership and a privilege.

Many of my friends who are leaders have developed strategies for investing in others daily. Real estate broker Dianna Kokoszka sets alerts on her phone twice a day. In the morning an alert pops up with this question: "Who will you add value to today?" At 8:00 p.m. the alert asks, "How did you add value to others today?" If she feels that she hasn't added value to someone that day, she doesn't go to bed until she has.

Entrepreneur and author Chris Estes sends a one-minute phone message of encouragement to five people every day. Businessman and EQUIP board member Collin Sewell writes three personal notes every day. You don't have to be a superstar or an overachiever to add value to people. You just need to care and begin doing something about it.

Identifying Your Sweet Spot

What is your purpose? Do you know what you were made for? And how can you tap into your sweet spot to help others and add value to them? If you are already an established leader, you may have leadership skills you can teach to others. But think beyond those skills to some of your other skills and to your resources. Who on your team struggles with an area that is a strength for you? How might they learn from you to improve in that area?

If you aren't experienced with adding value to others or are still not sure what your sweet spot is, that's okay. Adding value is a skill in itself. You can develop it. But that will happen only when you give it a try. Begin by doing your best to add value to a few people using the things you naturally do well, and keep fine-tuning your efforts until it aligns with your sweet spot.

The Five Essential Values of Adding Value to Others

Do you have the desire to help other people and add value to them? If so, is it intentional and strategic? Are you willing to cultivate the desire so that it is more pro-active? If so, there are five important insights about adding value to others that will help you. They helped strengthen my commitment to and vision of serving others, and I believe they will do the same for you.

1. To Add Value to Others I Must First Value Myself

As parents, Margaret and I realized when our children were young that we couldn't teach them everything, so we came up with five essential principles we wanted to pass along that would help them be successful and feel good about who they are. We wanted to ground them in faith, responsibility, unconditional love (so they would know what it's like to prosper and thrive), gratitude, and self-worth.

We included self-worth because we understood that it's impossible to consistently behave in a way that is inconsistent with how we feel about ourselves on the inside. Self-image dictates daily behavior. How we see ourselves regulates what we consistently do, and our regular behavior is what defines us, not what we might do on a rare occasion. The ability to add value to others has to be based on more than just saying, "I value people." It must be built upon the solid ground of believing in ourselves. The only way we can be consistent and authentic in valuing others is to see value in ourselves.

Observers of human behavior have learned that people with low self-esteem are almost always self-centered and preoccupied with their own thoughts and actions. In contrast, people who help others tend to feel good about the people they help and to feel good about themselves. When you add value to others, there is an instant return of positive emotions that causes you to feel better about who you are. Haven't you experienced those positive feelings when you've helped someone in need? Positive thinking doesn't build self-image. Positive acts do. There's nothing wrong with positive thinking, but if you perform positive acts, not only will your self-image begin to rise, you will find yourself living a more significant life that matters.

If you're wondering whether you value yourself enough to add value to others, then think about this. You know you truly value yourself when each day you silently affirm that you are the type of person with whom you would like to spend the rest of your life. If you don't feel that way, then you still have some work to do on the inside to be in the best position to help others.

2. To Add Value to Others I Must Value Others

Mother Teresa said, "One of the greatest diseases is to be nobody to anybody." As a pastor, I spent a lot of time visiting people in nursing homes over the years. One of the heartbreaks for me was the people I saw who never had family visiting them. *Does anybody even know they're here?* I'd wonder. *Does anyone even care?*

When I did weekly hospital visits, I would often check in with the front desk to see if there were any people who had not been visited by anyone since my last call. And I did my best to look in on those who'd had no visitors. I didn't always get to everyone, but I surely tried.

How often do we look past others, not really seeing who they are? Not getting to know them? Not valuing them as individuals? Every person has value, and to be people who live lives that matter, we need to intentionally value others and express that value to them. It's not optional if we desire to be significant.

3. To Add Value to Others I Must Value What Others Have Done for Me

One Thanksgiving a few years ago when our grandchildren were very young, Margaret and I decided to help them put on a Thanksgiving Day play for the whole family. Margaret was in charge of the costumes, I was the producer and director (I bet that's a surprise!), and the children were the talent. As I led them through rehearsal, they practiced their songs and memorized various inspirational quotes about Thanksgiving. Our grandson, little John, was five years old at the time. His only line was, "We all should have an attitude of gratitude."

The morning of the play he came to me to practice his line. He kept saying "gratitude" before "attitude." After a few times trying to get it right, he was flustered and tired. Falling down on the floor, he looked up at me and said, "This gratitude stuff is exhausting."

I laughed at his hilarious delivery, and then I immediately rewrote his part to include his statement with the dramatics of falling down. Later I thought, *Gratitude isn't supposed to be exhausting. It's supposed to be invigorating!* But of course, when we put gratitude before attitude, it can be exhausting.

If you don't have an attitude of gratitude on Thanksgiving Day, then it is going to be hard to be appreciative any day of the year. Gratitude is the motivation for doing good things for others, and a positive attitude is what drives that action. Gratitude fuels us to want to do good things for others.

Have you ever met people who think nothing good ever happens to them? It's like they walk around with dark clouds over their heads, and they always say things like, "No one ever gives me a chance. I never get a break. Why doesn't anyone ever pick me?" Such people live very self-consuming, selfish lives. How can they experience significance at all?

We've all heard the expression "Count your blessings." But have you ever stopped to wonder what that really means? When we count our blessings and realize what others have done for us, it stimulates us to say, "I want to do something for someone else." You have to count your blessings before you can be a blessing.

4. To Add Value to Others I Must Know and Relate to What Others Value

In this world, I believe we all have *one* thing we are really best at. For me, that's communication. I believe my strength in communication is being other-person focused, not focused on myself.

Early in my career, I came to the conclusion that all

great speakers lose themselves in their audience. They have one desire, and that is to connect with people. You can't connect with an audience if you're above them. If you look down on people, you won't want to raise them up. But that psychological truth also comes into play physically. I like being down where the people are, so whenever possible I get off the platform. I leave the stage and walk among the crowd. It takes away barriers. If you move toward people, they move toward you. If you move away from people, they pull back, too.

If you want to impress people, talk about your successes. But if you want to impact people, talk about your failures. Telling self-deprecating stories in a conversational style helps me get to a place where I can communicate with people in a way that makes them feel comfortable, without my coming off as authoritarian. And that's when I have the best chance of adding value to them. Everything I do when I speak is intentional. But I'm sure that does not come as a surprise. By now you know intentionality is a lifestyle I've practiced for many years.

In 2010 I wrote a book called *Everyone Communicates, Few Connect*. In it I describe connecting practices that we can use to better connect with others. The first connecting principle is to find common ground. When we first meet someone, there is a relationship gap between us. We don't know them, they don't know us.

Who will be the first to close that gap? The one who finds common ground. How do you do that? By embracing these seven qualities and practices:

- Availability—I will choose to spend time with others.
- Listening—I will listen my way to common ground.
- Questions—I will be interested enough in others to ask questions.
- Thoughtfulness—I will think of others and how to connect with them.
- Openness—I will let people into my life.
- Likability—I will care about people.
- Humility—I will think of myself less so I can think of others more.

Do you know and relate to what others value? Do you go out of your way to connect with others? It doesn't have to be anything big, and it doesn't have to be limited to the people you lead. You can connect with people everywhere in simple ways. Get to know your neighbors and do something nice for them. Learn the name of your waitress and leave her a good tip. Talk with children to find out what's important to them, and then praise and encourage them. Do what you can wherever you are.

5. To Add Value to Others I Must Make Myself More Valuable

The idea of adding value to people is dependent on the fact that you have something of value to give them. Adding value to someone is relatively easy to do once. But as a leader, you will want to add value to the people you lead consistently every day. To do that, you must continually grow and become more valuable. And to add the most value, you should try to stay in your sweet spot.

Each of us right now has a lid on our potential. The only way to lift that lid is to intentionally develop and grow. As you do this you will make a wonderful discovery—you can also lift the lids of others. I have always considered myself to be a lid lifter—someone who sees the greatest potential in others and then gives them what they need to rise up and fly.

I found this to be true in Lancaster. As I equipped and trained people to do specific tasks, I started to get additional opportunities to add value to them in other ways. I helped them to become better leaders. I challenged them to strive for excellence in other areas of their lives. I helped them improve the important relationships in their lives. And I supported them as they fought to strengthen their characters. Every time I learned a new skill or fought a personal battle, I had more to give. As I improved myself, I helped others to improve, too.

Grow yourself—grow others. Learn for yourself—then pass it on. Lift your lid so that you can lift others'!

Knowing How You Can Add Value

Do you agree that adding value to people, both as a leader and as an individual, has high value? Can you see that being intentional about it is a key to living a life of significance and having a life that matters? If so, then you're probably wondering *how* you should try to add value. To know the answer, ask yourself these three questions:

1. What Have I Been Given? (Looking Backward)

What experiences have you had that have uniquely equipped you to add value to others? Those experiences could be positive, or they could be difficulties or negative circumstances that you have overcome. I know people who have had eating disorders and were able to come alongside others who struggled with that same issue and help them. I've known people who have made fortunes who used their money to build villages, rescue orphans, and construct hospitals. I know people with a knack for business who have helped budding entrepreneurs in developing countries.

What accomplishments, resources, and experiences

can you draw upon? What wisdom have you gained through the crucible of personal loss or tragedy? What can you draw upon to help others and add value to them?

2. What Do I Have to Give? (Looking Inward)

Everyone has qualities, talents, and skills that have the potential to add value to others. What is inside you that can help you make others better? What skills do you possess? What talents have been given to you? What personality traits do you have that can be used to add value to others? *Anything* and *everything* you have can be used to help others if you make adding value to people your priority and become intentional about it.

3. What Can I Do? (Looking Outward)

So often we only see what we are prepared to see in others. But looking outward with an eagerness to add value to others changes how we see those same people. Ideally, it will inspire us to invest in others daily.

Every day I can be intentional in adding value to people's lives. Every day I can look at my schedule and ask myself, "Who can I help today? How can I help them? When should I do that?" You can do that same thing. You can approach the day looking for the potential in the people around you and opportunities for adding value to them.

In Lancaster I started where I was with the people I

had, teaching them what I knew. I immediately began training them to do things they wanted to do. That became my main focus. And I developed a process that I still use to this day:

Model—I do it. Before I try to teach someone else, I work to become good at it so that I know what I'm doing.

Mentor—I do it and you watch. Learning begins when I show someone how to do what I do. I learned in Lancaster never to work alone. No matter what task I was doing, I always tried to take with me someone who wanted to learn.

Monitor—You do it and I watch. Nobody learns how to do something well on the first try. People need to be coached. When others do the task and I'm there to watch, I can help them troubleshoot problems and improve.

Motivate—You do it. I always try to hand off tasks as soon as possible and encourage the people I've trained. I become their biggest cheerleader.

Multiply—You do it and someone else is with you. This is the final step. I don't want the equipping cycle to end with me. I want it to continue. When I train someone to do something, I want them to turn around and train someone else, just as I did them.

Who is already in your life that you can add value to? What can you do to help them? Opportunities are all around you. All you have to do is be willing to act. What do you have to give? What can you help someone on your team learn? How can you make life better for others? What you have to give is unique. What's your sweet spot? No one else can give what you can give.

We can all add value to people. And the biggest difference we can make will come from our sweet spot. We should not leave what we do best. We should stay with our best to give our best—and make the greatest impact.

There is a passage in the book *Souls on Fire* by Elie Wiesel in which he writes that when you die and you meet your Maker, you're not going to be asked why you didn't become a Messiah or find a cure for cancer. All you're going to be asked is, "Why didn't you become you? Why didn't you become all that you are?" To become all you are, you must use your best to add value to people.

Intentional Application

What Do You Have to Offer?

There are several ways to examine your life to discover how to add value from your sweet spot. Right now I'd like to offer two. One is analytical; the other is intuitive. First, the analytical method: use the perspective outlined in the chapter to determine how you can add value:

- *Look backward—what have I been given?* What unique experiences and resulting insights can you use to add value to others?
- *Look inward—what do I have to give?* What talents, strengths, and skills do you possess that you can use to add value to others?
- *Look outward—what can I do?* What can you do *daily* to add value to others?

Write your answers to these questions. Then become determined to leverage what you have for others *every day.*

If that method doesn't suit you, then try the intuitive method: pay attention to what you feel when you help people. When I add value to people by communicating with them, especially on the subject of leadership, it resonates within me.

What resonates within you? When do you possess the sense that you were made to do a particular thing? Take time to brainstorm any and every moment in your life when you *felt* you were doing what you were meant to do. Write down each of those moments, what you were doing, and what exactly resonated in you. Then spend time reflecting on them until you can see a pattern or otherwise make some sense of it.

6

Partnering with Like-Valued People

In 1987 I turned forty. I saw this birthday as a major milestone, so I approached it as an athlete would half-time. I saw it as an opportunity to check the scoreboard of my life, assess my performance, analyze my deficiencies, and begin making adjustments before going back out on the field to play my second half. In the eyes of others, I had accomplished some major achievements. But when I stopped to examine my life, I was not satisfied. I felt there was something greater I wasn't doing.

The Next Steps in My Journey

To help you understand this, I need to catch you up on my story and tell you what I was doing during the ten years before my fortieth birthday. Margaret and I left Lancaster in 1979. Why would we leave people we loved, a church where we were making a difference, and an area where we felt at home? That's a fair question.

We were highly successful in Lancaster, but I began to want to do more. And I started to wonder if the leadership principles I was developing and the values I was embracing could be used in organizations I wasn't leading myself. In other words, I wondered if I could make a difference beyond my personal reach, through other leaders I trained in other parts of the country. Could I make a more significant impact?

I got a chance to test that idea when I was offered a position with another ministry organization at their national office. The new position would allow me to spend all of my time training pastors in churches around the country who were part of that organization. Margaret and I packed up Elizabeth and Joel, our two young children, and we moved to central Indiana.

The good news was that I discovered that the leadership ideas I had developed in Hillham and Lancaster *did* transfer. They really worked for anyone who valued leadership and was willing to become a better leader. Every leader I worked with who put my principles into practice was more successful. But there was also a downside. I was limited in whom I could help since I was allowed to work only with people in that one organization. I wanted to reach more people, and that made me realize that the best place for me to do that was as the pastor of a local church. When I got the invitation to lead Skyline (the church I mentioned in chapter 3), I gladly accepted, and our family moved from Indiana to California. That was in 1981.

The first thing I started doing when we got there was to get the church, which had plateaued, growing again. The task of building a great church was familiar territory for me. I understood that world and knew what it would take. I rebuilt the staff, changed how we did things, and found creative ways to reach out into the community. It wasn't long before Skyline was recognized as one of the most influential churches in America by Elmer Towns, a church growth expert and college professor whom I admired and who became a good friend.

In the early 1980s I also started teaching leadership conferences outside of the church. When I took the position at Skyline, the board understood that I wanted to add value to other leaders, and they agreed to give me the flexibility to do that. When I was invited to start speaking for a training organization, I chose to teach R-E-A-L, the four things every person needs to be successful: relationships, equipping, attitude, and leadership.

Before long, I realized I wanted to emphasize leadership more in my communication, so I created a company called INJOY and started hosting my own conferences. To say that I believed big but started small would be an understatement. The first leadership conference I hosted myself was in Kansas City, Missouri. Only fourteen people signed up for it, and I stood to lose a couple thousand dollars if I went through with it. A friend told me doing it would be a bad business decision. But I could see that it would be a good *significance* decision, so I did it anyway.

That was the first of what became many dozens of conferences I ended up holding. Eventually hundreds and then thousands would attend and learn how to become better leaders. I wouldn't have described it this way at that time, but what I was really teaching leaders was intentional living.

At a small conference in a Holiday Inn in Jackson, Mississippi, a group of leaders told me that they were grateful for what I had taught them during the conference, but they wanted ongoing training. I wasn't sure what to do, but I wanted to help them. I could tell they wanted to make a difference. Have you ever been in a situation like that, where you felt compelled to do something, but you weren't sure how to make it happen?

Then I had a thought. I asked, "If I created a one-hour training tape every month, would you sign up for it as a subscription?" They said yes, so I passed a legal pad around the room to get their information. All thirty-five attendees signed up for it. That's how my monthly leadership tape club was born. That small list of people eventually exploded into more than fifteen thousand subscribers, with each tape being listened to by an average of five people. I was thrilled, because I was adding value to leaders, and they were multiplying that value to others.

The Key to the Next Level

So by the time I turned forty, I had done a lot. When I looked at each of the things I had accomplished, I was happy with it. I felt what I had done had made a difference. So why was I feeling dissatisfied? Why wasn't I pleased? Why wasn't what I'd done enough? What had I missed?

That's when it hit me. I hadn't developed a team. There was no way I could be any more productive as an individual. For twenty years I'd found new and better ways to get more done. But I was at the limit. If I could develop a team, *we* could be more productive. Not only that, but we could do things *better* than I could do alone. I was living in *me* world, and I needed to be living in *we* world.

Had I been training leaders? Yes. Had I been including others in my significance journey? Yes. But had I been truly developing my team and partnering with them? No.

This became the birthday that challenged me to make major changes in the way I did things. The change in my thinking was huge. It was in the top half-dozen most important decisions I ever made. And it was *the* most important business decision of my life. I finally understood that life isn't made by what you can accomplish. It's made by what you can accomplish with others.

From this point on in my life, every decision I made focused on developing others. And before long it began compounding. Not only did I accomplish more, but my team accomplished more. I watched as they developed as people. And I discovered that I actually found greater joy in seeing them succeed than I did in succeeding myself. Wow! What a change that was for me.

I also began to develop my staff in new ways. How could I travel often to train and develop other leaders yet still lead the church effectively? By developing great leaders who could lead without me. I partnered with Dan Reiland, who became my executive pastor; Steve Babby, who oversaw finances; and Tim Elmore, who did research and developed sermon outlines that he and I both taught. Every key person I partnered with shared the same values I did. But each had his or her own personality and skill set that contributed to the bigger vision to make a difference.

Out of this discovery came what later became the Law of the Inner Circle in *The 21 Irrefutable Laws of Leadership.* It states, "A leader's potential is determined by those closest to him." The reason I have been successful in the years since my fortieth birthday is that I understand this law, and every decision I've made since then has been based on finding like-valued people, developing their potential, and partnering with them to accomplish a shared vision.

The Power of Partnership

Partnership with like-valued people is powerful. Perhaps the best way for me to explain it is to recount a conversation I had not long ago with a small group of leaders from Latin America. The eighteen men and women I was meeting with collectively had forty-five to fifty million people under their leadership. Although each of them was already extremely successful, none was hitting 100 percent of his or her capacity. By my estimation, almost every person in the room was averaging somewhere between 75 and 80 percent. My goal that day was to show them how to move up to the next level of impact.

When I asked the group their thoughts on how to make that happen, every answer they gave would have yielded only a very modest increase in their effectiveness—their best idea adding perhaps at most a 5 percent increase.

This was a sophisticated group of achievers, yet they didn't give the answer that I knew was the key. I believed that if they'd been aware of the answer, they would have already been practicing it. I could sense that they were getting restless, so I finally gave them the solution. "Partnerships," I said.

The room fell silent. It wasn't at all what they were expecting. But they got it immediately. We went on to have a great discussion of partnership and to trade ideas about potential partners.

Here's the most important thing to know about partnerships and alliances: to be effective, they must be made with like-minded but—more importantly—*like-valued* people. If you aren't connecting and partnering with people who share your dream *and* values, you have no shot at making these partnerships work.

Having the right partners will help you gain momentum and build your dream into something bigger. There's great strength in numbers. As the old adage says, two heads are better than one. Partnering with a community of like-valued people will help you multiply whatever dream you have of making a difference.

A community helps us go farther, and when it's a community of talented, like-valued, complementary people, we can actually go faster, too. Great partnerships make you better than you are, multiply your value, enable you to do what you do best, allow you to help others do their best, give you more time, provide you with companionship, help you fulfill the desires of your heart, and compound your vision and effort.

The moment you partner with somebody, you tap into something you've never had access to before. You gain their knowledge, experience, influence, and potential. When you are already achieving at a highly effective level, you don't gain a great increase by getting significantly better yourself. You gain it by partnering or connecting with other good people who bring something different to the table. And that makes you better. If the partnerships you make are with like-valued people, there's no limit to the difference you can make!

Many things can bring people together in the short term: passion, opportunity, urgency, convenience. However, if a partnership is to last over the long haul, there must be shared values. When people's values are different, there will inevitably be a parting of the ways.

It's important to know what you're looking for when it comes to shared values. Most people miss opportunities in life, not because the opportunity wasn't there, but because they didn't have a clue what it looked like when it arrived. They never took the time to figure out what they were looking for. It's all about intentionality. You have to know what you're looking for if you want to find it.

Finding the Right Partners

Early in my career, I had no clear picture of who I was looking for—not when I entered the pastorate and not when I entered the business world. When I got started in my business life, I made some decisions to hire people who weren't the right fit. I had a blind spot when it came to people. I thought the best of everyone and couldn't always see people for who they really were. Despite those in my inner circle warning me and cautioning me, I always wanted to give people the benefit of the doubt. That got me into trouble more than once.

Since the picture of who I needed wasn't clear, I then allowed others to paint the picture for me. Invariably, they always painted *their* pictures. Then I discovered that the pictures they had painted of themselves had been greatly enhanced. They were like the glamour shots people take and then doctor in Photoshop.

How do I compensate for this now? I build in a 10 percent exaggeration factor.

The way this works became clear to me on the golf course. Bear with me for a moment, and you'll understand what I mean. Most golfers, you see, exaggerate their skills. It starts when they give their handicap. Unless they're sandbagging to try to win a bet, they typically overestimate their ability. Their best golf moment is on the first tee when they share their golf handicap. Then they hit the ball and their true game shows up.

Golfers make the same mistake when they select a club during a round. Most golfers check their yardage, then select their club based on how far the ball would go if they hit a true shot with that club 100 percent of the time. Maybe one time they hit their 8 iron 150 yards with a pure swing. The rest of the time they hit it 135 yards. Their ball is lying at 150 yards, so what club do they choose? The 8 iron—the club they think they *should* hit 150 yards, not the club they actually *do* hit 150 yards with most of the time.

When I select a club for a shot, I subtract 10 percent of my distance from a perfect shot. In a round I may hit one 100 percent perfect shot, but I will hit twenty-five 90 percent shots. I select my clubs based upon what I most often do, not what I have done only once or twice in my whole life. Wrong club selection is the number one mistake of amateur golfers who hit the ball short of the hole.

When partnering with people, don't choose based on what they *say* they can do, or based on what they did *once*. Choose based on their regular behaviors. That's what tells you what their values are. Too often our choices are made by what we *could* or think we *should* do rather than what we *usually* do. We are all human, so we should give everyone the benefit of the doubt. But we also need to be realistic. We need to have a picture of what we're shooting for.

The Twelve Qualities of People Who Make a Difference

If you're looking for people to join you in making a meaningful difference in the world, what do you look for? I've taken the time to identify what I look for in people when I am seeking to partner with them. I believe that this list will help you as you seek out people to partner with to achieve your goals.

1. Good Partners Think of Others before Themselves

My favorite description of humility is this: people who are humble don't think less of themselves; they just think of themselves less. Maturity isn't growing older, nor getting wiser. It is developing the ability to see things from another person's point of view. When you combine humility with maturity you have the ideal person that I want to partner with, and probably the kind of like-valued person you want to look for, too. I'm drawn to people who understand that with one tiny exception, the world is composed of others.

2. Good Partners Think Bigger than Themselves

People who want to make a difference have expanded their worlds over the years from *me* to *we*. They have broken out of their selfish what's-in-it-for-me mind-sets and have stretched beyond their own needs first. Their dreams now include helping others and reaching across fences to show that they are their brother's keepers. They are grateful for the opportunity to serve their communities. They always approach others with a win-win mind-set and always cross the finish line as relay team members, not single sprinters.

3. Good Partners Have a Passion That's Contagious

The people I want to partner with have a love for people and life that can be easily felt by everyone around them. When they walk into a room, their presence is palpably positive. Others are energized by their spirits, lifted by their love, and valued by their actions. To know them is to want to be around them. Their presence marks others and soon, everyone is inspired to live on a higher level so they, too, can pass on the joys of significant living to others.

4. Good Partners Have Complementary Gifts

Mother Teresa said, "I cannot do what you can do. You cannot do what I can do. Together we can do great things." Nothing is more rewarding than a common mission being achieved by people with complementary gifts working together in harmony. For years, the members of my inner circle have made me better because they are gifted differently than I am. Each person brings something unique to the table, and they are not afraid to share their knowledge or perspectives. Their presence adds value to everything I do. No one is the total package. But if you put the right group of people together, you can create the total package.

5. Good Partners Connect and Provide Great Support

You can't genuinely partner with people when you're not connected with them. Besides, today we live in a world of connections. There was a time when people could retreat to their own little castles, each surrounded by a moat to protect their privacy, and try to live in isolation. Today the moats are dried up.

Partners need to connect, and they need to support one another. Some of my closest friends are those who help me carry out my mission every day. Our worlds are forever linked. I often ask myself, *What would I do without them?* The answer is, *Not much.*

6. Good Partners Show a Can-Do Creative Spirit about Challenges

If we want to fulfill our dreams and live out our *whys*, we need to partner with people who have a can-do spirit. Not everyone possesses that. When faced with obstacles, people have different responses. There are...

- **"I Can't" People:** They are convinced that they can't, so they won't and don't.
- **"I Don't Think I Can" People:** These people might be able to, but they talk themselves out of it. As a result they fulfill their words by not trying.
- **"Can I?" People:** These individuals allow their doubts to control their actions, which can lead to failure.
- **"How Can I?" People:** These people have already made the decision to tackle their tough assignments.

The only substantial question they struggle with is how they are going to do it.

This last group is my kind of people. Why? Because when we work together, *everything* is possible. It may take a while, but the vision will be accomplished.

7. Good Partners Expand Our Influence

For more than forty years I have taught that leadership is influence. During those years I have intentionally expanded my influence with others because I know it allows me to make a greater difference in the world. However, twenty years ago I made a great discovery. When I partner with like-valued people, I go from increasing to multiplying my influence.

Successful people understand that working hard at networking with other people is time well spent. It's the quickest and best way to find partners and opportunities to expand our influence.

8. Good Partners Are Activists

People who are willing to take a stand for what they believe in have an inherent bias toward action. There is no "ready, aim, aim, aim...fire" in their lives. If they err, it's on the side of "ready, fire, aim."

Activists don't merely accept their lives as they are; they lead their lives. They take things where they want them to go. They live their stories—100 percent. Nothing less is good enough for them. Every day they maximize opportunity and seize the chance to make their day a masterpiece.

9. Good Partners Are Ladder Builders, Not Ladder Climbers

My friend Sam Chand, the speaker and consultant, taught me the difference between ladder climbers and ladder builders. He says, "We all start out life climbing our own ladders and living for ourselves. Over time, some people begin to shift from climbing to their own success, and they start building ladders for others to climb."

Sam has built a lot of ladders for others, including me. He's my kind of guy because he has dedicated his life to climbing with others toward a life of significance. If you want to make a difference, look for people like him.

10. Good Partners Are Head and Shoulders above the Crowd

The kinds of people I enjoy partnering with are easy to find. Why do I say that? Because they stand out from others. They take action when others won't. They add value to others every day. And their growth as human beings is dramatic as a result of intentionally making a difference in the lives of others. The only time you can't see them is when they're stooping down to help someone else.

My kinds of people want others to do better than they do, so that they, too, can rise higher and accomplish more. Metaphorically, they allow others to stand on their shoulders. They are record setters who want to help others break their own records. As you look for partners who will help you make a difference, search for those who stand out in a crowd.

11. Good Partners Provide Synergy That Gives a High Return

When you partner with the right person, it's like $1 + 1 = 3$. There is a synergy that comes when the right people are working together. It's similar to what happens when a group of horses work together. Maybe you've heard about that. For example, two horses can pull about nine thousand pounds together. How many pounds can four horses pull? Without synergy, you'd do the math and assume the answer is eighteen thousand pounds. That would be reasonable, but it would be wrong. Four horses working together can actually pull over thirty thousand pounds.

When it comes to partnerships, synergy enables the group to outperform even its best individual members. That teamwork will produce an overall better result than if each person within the group was working toward the same goal individually. What can't be accomplished when there's synergy and commitment involved? United you can do much, much more!

12. Good Partners Make a Difference in Us

When I started partnering with other people, it was my intent that together we would make a difference for others. What surprised me was that the partnerships also made such a great difference for me. I discovered it is much more fun to do things together. But more important, I became a better person because of those who came alongside me.

As you seek out the right people to develop partnerships with, I need to let you know what the best foundation is for building a good partnership: similar capacity. Partnerships are lost more out of mismatched capacity than anything else. A solid partnership comes together because two people have something to offer each other, and what they give and receive are equally valued. It works like a scale. If one person is doing more giving than the other, then the partnership becomes unbalanced and it becomes strained. For the partnership to last, it has to come back into some kind of balance where the two feel the give-and-take works for both of them. And if the partnership is going to last, as it goes down the road and it grows, adapts, and evolves, both members must be able to change and adjust. If they don't, it will end. As long as each partner continues adding value to the other and as long as there is capacity on both sides, the partnership can blossom.

Most times when you enter into a partnership, you don't know in advance how it will go or if it will last. For it to have a chance, you have to spend a lot of connecting time with your partner, nurturing the relationship like any other. If you don't nurture that relationship, it's like any other living thing you ignore: it dies. Partnership starts with finding common ground and common goals. From there it builds from the relational to the inspirational.

And you have to remember that partnerships are more like movies than photographs. They change from moment to moment. Only time lets you know what's coming next. Capacity can't be predicted any more than trust can. But if you share intentionality, if you share vision, if you have common goals and a common purpose, if you're moving in the same direction, and if you are like-minded and like-valued, you've got a pretty good shot at making the partnership work. A strong partnership divides the effort and multiplies the effect. And if both keep giving, it has a shot at lasting.

Whatever your passion is, think about how your

effectiveness could be multiplied if you started connecting and partnering with the *right* people. Whatever difference you're able to make will be multiplied.

Every person who has partnered with me over the years on this significance journey deserves credit, just as everyone who partners with you will deserve it. As you look for like-valued people to partner with, make sure they possess what I call "the great separators." All of my most effective partners shared these qualities that make a difference. They possessed commitment. I always asked for that up front, because commitment separates the players from the pretenders. They thought beyond themselves, because to make a difference, people have to put others first. They had the capacity to dream big dreams. I wanted to partner with people who thought without limitations. And they possessed passion. This was most important, because passion is contagious and influences others. It invites energy and it creates movement.

Perhaps at the time I could not have told you that these were the exact things I was looking for, because I didn't have enough experience yet to articulate them. But I followed my intuition. I sensed that much more energy was required to do something significant. And I knew I'd need a group of like-valued people around me—people who wanted to make a difference.

Teaming up with other people who want to make a

difference is the multiplying factor that makes it possible for an individual to change a family, a community, a city, a country—the world. If you have a vision of significance that promises to help other people, and you partner with others who share that same vision, there is no limit to what can be done.

In our busy and hectic lives, it is sometimes easy for us to overlook or forget the power of partnership. However, when you live with intentional significance, your inclusion of others also has to become intentional. As you make plans, you must involve other people and invite them not just to follow you as a leader, but also to become your partners. To receive their full engagement, you must be ready to commit, compromise, sacrifice, and connect with them. You don't get more than you give. But when you give those things, they are likely to reciprocate. And there's an amazing and powerful compounding effect that takes place.

Intentional Application

What Are Your Values?

To find like-valued people, it helps to know what you're looking for. Take some time to think about the values most important to you for making a difference in the lives of others. Write them down.

Now begin looking for people who share your values. When you find them, connect with them. Start building your relationships with them so that you're ready to take the next step, which is to look for ways to work together to make a difference.

EPILOGUE

The Making of a Movement

Right now are you only dreaming about making a difference, or are you actually doing things to connect with people who can join you on the significance journey? Movements don't begin with the masses—they always start with one, and then they attract others to themselves and their causes.

Anyone on the planet today can make a difference with others. You can, I can, and even the guy or gal sitting next to you on the plane, bus, or subway can. Movements are about mobilizing people to get behind a shared purpose. There is great power in helping other people because you can change the way people think, believe, and even live. And that group of people can end up changing their culture, if not the world.

Today I have another dream. I want to see people become

intentional in their living. I want to see them become transformational leaders who influence others to think, speak,
and act in such a way that it makes a positive difference.
Will it become a movement? I don't know. I have no control
over that. I only have control over myself. I know that it has
to start with me, and I feel moved to share it with you.

This book is my invitation for you to join me. I want
you to embrace these ideas, and for the story of your life
to change, as mine has. I want you to take action to make
a positive difference in the lives of others. I want you
to connect and partner with others and achieve significance. And my hope, someday, is to hear a million stories of changed lives because people like you and me
tried to make a difference for others.

If you join me in my dream, maybe together we can
help create a world where people think of others before
themselves, where adding value to others is a priority,
where financial gain is secondary to future potential,
and where your self-worth is strengthened by acts of
significance every day. It's my dream. I hope one day
it becomes our reality. But it can come to be only if we
connect with others and work together.

Leading with Purpose

Now you know how to live a life of purpose with others,
I want to ask you a series of questions. See how many
you can honestly answer yes to:

- Are you choosing to live a story of significance?
- Are you seizing opportunities and taking action to make a difference?
- Have you put other people first to make a difference?
- Are you connecting with like-minded people who make a difference?
- Are you trying to add value to others from your sweet spot to make a difference?
- Are you trying to partner with like-valued people to make a difference?

If you answered yes to all of these questions—or if you are willing to answer yes and take action *now*—then you have crossed over into the significant life, and you are a leader. You will make a difference. Your life will matter. And you will start to change the world. You've made the decision. Now you just need to manage that decision every day of your life. You just need to keep living with purpose and take action in some small way every day.

Notes

1. Donald Miller, *A Million Miles in a Thousand Years: What I Learned While Editing My Life* (Nashville: Thomas Nelson, 2009), 236–37.
2. Luke 22:27, MSG.

About the Author

John C. Maxwell is a #1 *New York Times* bestselling author, coach, and speaker who has sold more than twenty-nine million books in fifty languages. In 2014 he was identified as the #1 leader in business by the American Management Association® and the most influential leadership expert in the world by *Business Insider* and *Inc.* magazine. He is the founder of The John Maxwell Company, The John Maxwell Team, EQUIP, and the John Maxwell Leadership Foundation, organizations that have trained millions of leaders. In 2015 they reached the milestone of having trained leaders from every country of the world. The recipient of the Mother Teresa Prize for Global Peace and Leadership from the Luminary Leadership Network, Dr. Maxwell speaks each year to *Fortune* 500 companies, presidents of nations, and many of the world's top business leaders. He can be followed at Twitter.com/JohnCMaxwell. For more information about him visit JohnMaxwell.com.

If you want further guidance in exploring
your purpose, look for

THE POWER OF SIGNIFICANCE

How Purpose Changes Your Life

We all have a longing to be significant, to make a contribution, to be
a part of something noble and purposeful. In *The Power of Significance*, John Maxwell gives practical guidance and motivation to get
you started on your unique personal path to significance. Learn how
to find your why, start small but believe big, seize great opportunities, and live every day as if it matters—because it does!

Available now from Center Street wherever books are sold.

Also available in Spanish and from ⊡ hachette and ⊡ hachette

John Maxwell's Bestselling Successful People Series—Over 1 Million Copies Sold

WHAT SUCCESSFUL PEOPLE KNOW ABOUT LEADERSHIP

Advice from America's #1 Leadership Authority

The best leaders strive constantly to learn and grow, and every leader faces challenges. Discover actionable advice and solutions, as John Maxwell answers the most common leadership questions he receives.

HOW SUCCESSFUL PEOPLE THINK

Change Your Thinking, Change Your Life

Good thinkers are always in demand. They solve problems, never lack ideas, and always have hope for a better future. In this compact read, Maxwell reveals eleven types of successful thinking, and how you can maximize each to revolutionize your work and life.

HOW SUCCESSFUL PEOPLE LEAD

Taking Your Influence to the Next Level

True leadership is not generated by your title. In fact, being named to a position is the lowest of the five levels every effective leader achieves. Learn how to be more than a boss people are required to follow, and extend your influence beyond your immediate reach for the benefit of others.

HOW SUCCESSFUL PEOPLE GROW

15 Ways to Get Ahead in Life

John Maxwell explores the principles that are proven to be the most effective catalysts for personal growth. You can learn what it takes to strengthen your self-awareness, broaden your prospects, and motivate others with your positive influence.

HOW SUCCESSFUL PEOPLE WIN

Turn Every Setback into a Step Forward

No one wins at everything. But with this book John Maxwell will help you identify the invaluable life lessons that can be drawn from disappointing outcomes so you can turn every loss into a gain.

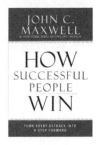

MAKE TODAY COUNT

The Secret of Your Success Is Determined by Your Daily Agenda

How can you know if you're making the most of today so you can have a better tomorrow? By following the twelve daily disciplines Maxwell describes in this book to give maximum impact in minimum time.

GET YOUR FREE MENTORING CALL
WITH
JOHN C. MAXWELL

Start setting goals to blow past your capacity today with a FREE mentoring call with John C. Maxwell. He'll equip you with the tools and practical thinking that will kick-start your journey to bigger goals, a better plan, and an intentional life.

GET IN-THE-MOMENT WISDOM FROM THE LEADERSHIP EXPERT

BREAKAWAY FOR A TAKEAWAY WITH DR. JOHN C. MAXWELL

Sign up today to get the most up-to-date and in-the-moment thoughts from John delivered right to your inbox. As you endeavor toward your biggest dreams and most daunting challenges, don't go it alone.

Receive relevant wisdom and practical insights from John as you

+ Discover your purpose
+ Navigate change
+ Expand your influence
+ Grow daily
+ Live fully
+ Experience lasting significance

PLUS VIP ACCESS TO EVENTS, SPECIAL OFFERS AND EXCLUSIVE UPDATES FROM JOHN!

MINUTE
WITH MAXWELL

Join me each and every day for "A Minute with Maxwell" as I inspire, challenge, and equip you with leadership teachings to apply to your lif and career. I am excited to share my short, powerful, FREE video messages with YOU.

Words are vital to communication and leadership. "A Minute with Maxwell" will grow YOUR library of leadership words! Words like *teamwork*, *potential*, *strive*, *connection*, *clarity*—to name a few!

SO WHAT ARE YOU WAITING FOR?
www.JohnMaxwellTeam.com

EQUIP®

Mobilizing Christian Leaders to Transform Their World

**FIND OUT
MORE HERE**

www.iequip.church
678.225.3300

People at all levels of an organization, not just the C-suite, have the ability to become effective leaders with proper training and commitment.

When you begin to invest in your human capital, watch what happens. Your workforce becomes aligned with your corporate initiatives. They begin supporting critical business priorities and change efforts, AND your business success begins to accelerate.

LEADERSHIP DEVELOPMENT   **EMPLOYEE ENGAGEMENT**   **CHANGE MANAGEMENT**

DOWNLOAD OUR FREE INFOGRAPHIC!
24 Proven Practices to Increase Employee Engagement
info.johnmaxwellcompany.com/increase-employee-engagement

The JOHN MAXWELL **Co.**
CORPORATE SOLUTIONS DIVISION

To learn more about our corporate training programs, contact our Corporate Solutions Division.
Visit **johnmaxwellcompany.com** *or call* **678-387-2810**.